Getting to know ...
Secret Lancashire

Ron and Marlene Freethy

RINTWISE PUBLICATIONS LIMITED
1992

This Edition
© Printwise Publication Ltd 1992   0556387/9

All photographs © Ron Freethy

Published by Printwise Publication Ltd
47 Bradshaw Road, Tottington, Bury, Lancs, BL8 3PW.

Warehouse and Orders
40-42 Willan Industrial Estate, Vere Street,
(Off Eccles New Road)
Salford, M5 2GR.
Tel: 061-745 9168   Fax: 061-737 1755

ISBN No 1 872226 53 1

Front cover photograph: Towneley Hall
Back cover photograph: Cottages near Lake Burwains

Edited by

_liff Hayes

Printed and bound by Manchester Free Press,
Paragon Mill, Jersey Street
Manchester, M4 6FP
Tel: 061 236 8822.

Introduction & Acknowledgements

We have been walking the highways and byways of Lancashire and the North Country for more than 30 years. We define ourselves more as strollers than walkers as we need time, often lots of time, to explore the history and natural history of the area through which we are passing.

We were pleased when Cliff Hayes suggested that we produce this book of strolls suitable for those who enjoy a meal in a hotel or taking a picnic. We were invited to update some walks which we published in the early 1980s and which have now changed for the better. The present book is dedicated to those who are frightened by maps and long strenuous walks but who love being out in the open air in beautiful countryside.

We are grateful to friends who suggested new walks which are included here or who allowed us to use their photographs when our own library proved lacking. To Carole Pugh we are grateful for the exquisite drawings.

Our thanks are also due to the Editor of the Lancashire Evening Telegraph who, over the last 23 years has published Freethy's Countryscene, a weekly feature and which has ensured that we have to do at least one walk each week. Some of this material is included in the present volume.

Finally we thank one energetic black labrador who insists that we walk throughout the year and in all weathers — a sure way to discover the secrets of an area.

Ron and Marlene Freethy

Lancashire as a county has a higher density of population and industry than almost any other. The fact that so much of its natural history remains and so many of its secret places have avoided being swamped is a tribute to its resilience. This and our companion volumes on the county are our tribute to "Lovely old Lanky"

About the Authors

Ron Freethy

Ron Freethy is President of the North East Lancashire Rambler's Association and has made many television and radio programmes. With his wife Marlene he has written several walking books and volumes on tourism throughout the country. The couple live in the Pendle area and are thus an ideal choice to prepare this book and the companion volumes.

Marlene Freethy with Bono ... always an excuse for a walk

*Samlesbury Chapel
– off the beaten
track, but well
worth a visit.*

Contents

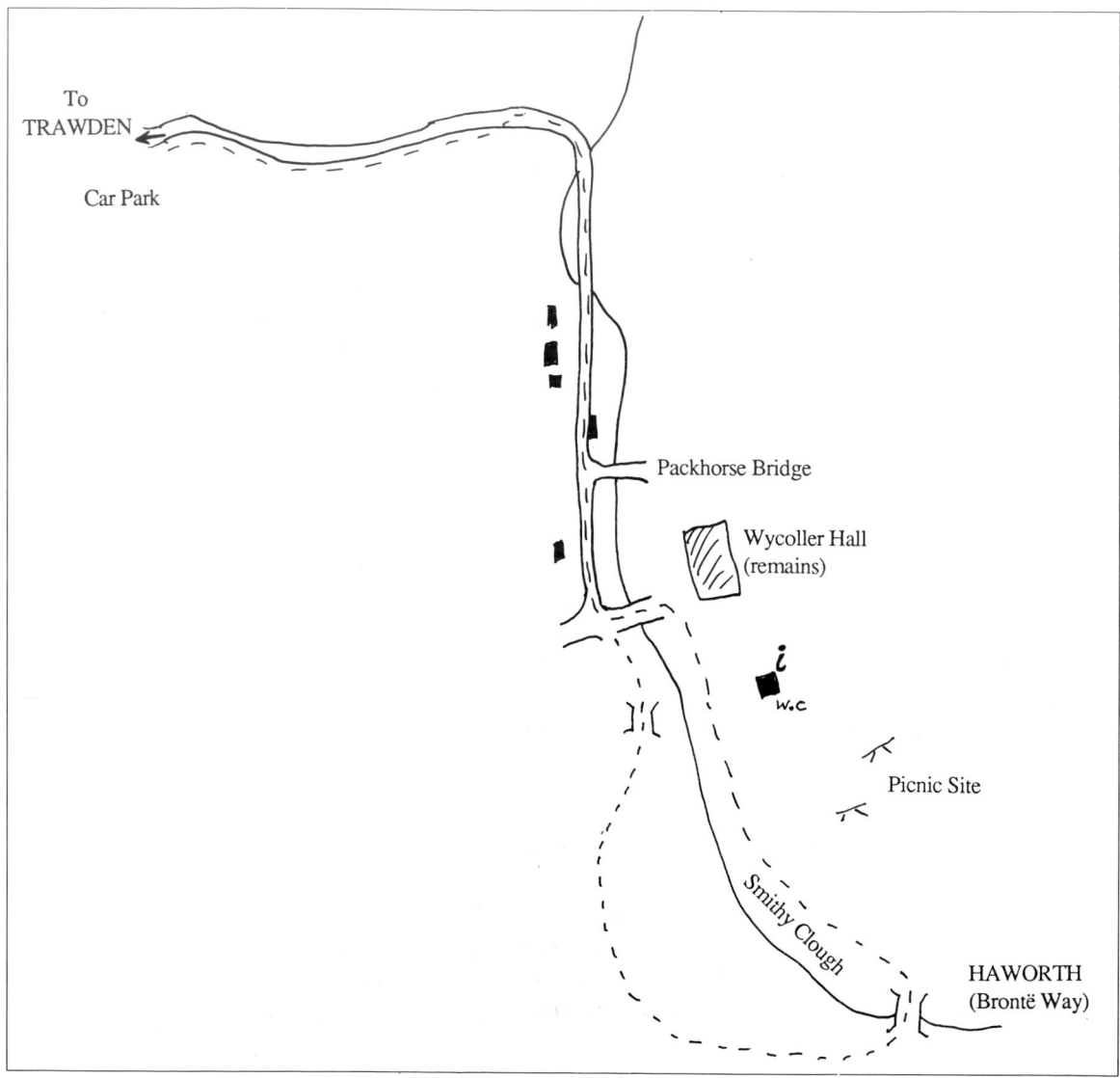

Walk One
Around Wycoller

ACCESS:
From Colne follow the A6068 towards Keighley as far as Laneshawbridge. Turn right signed Haworth. Cross a small bridge and then turn immediate right along Carriers Row. A series of well signed left turns leads to the Wycoller Country Park Car Park.

ROUTE:
From the car park, descend the steep road to the old village and approach the packhorse and clapper bridges. Keep these on the left and follow the marked footpath through a picnic area. This meets the main track. Turn left and pass the Information Centre on the right. Cross either the packhorse or the clapper bridge and return to the car park. The return path is very steep and disabled visitors are allowed to park in the village itself.

OUR WALK:
Allow at least two hours to explore the village and enjoy this stroll.

In the last few years Wycoller Country Park has developed quickly and from the village a spider's web of paths lead along streams, up hills, down dales and around farms. From the car park we followed the gentle slope down the well made path into the village. Although there is no public house in

Around Wycoller

the area there are a couple of excellent tea shops and plenty of picnic tables and seats.

We began our stroll in bright spring sunshine and by the time we reached the village it felt warm enough to be high summer. By the streamside we found a pair of mating frogs whilst other pairs had already started spawning in the shallow waters.

Sitting on the packhorse bridge were a group of Americans clutching copies of Charlotte Brontë's Jane Eyre and reading the section relating to Ferndean Manor which is said to have been based upon Wycoller Hall. There are ghost stories associated with the hall and may well also have inspired Anne Brontë's novel *The Tenant of Wildfell Hall.* The sisters were at

opposite:
Wycollar (as it was spelled in 1903) when it was more deserted than it is today. The hall is on the left with the clapper bridge to the right.

Wycoller Hall, used as inspiration by the Brontë sisters who knew it well

the peak of their writing in the 1840s and what they would have achieved had they been spared to live long lives we can but wonder in astonishment.

Although Wycoller Hall is a ruin it has retained its wonderful atmosphere and can be freely explored at leisure. As we entered the ruin we disturbed a group of four rabbits which ran away and uphill, their white tails bobbing and flashing in the sunlight. This was somewhat prophetic as the Cunliffe family badge incorporates a coney which was the old name for the rabbit. Their hall was built in the 1550s during the reign of Mary Tudor, the fiercely Catholic daughter of Henry VIII, and the sister of the equally fierce Protestant Elizabeth 1st. Wycoller has its ghost, but the galloping horseman is not likely to be encountered on a mild spring morning. The spirit hunter should return on a wild winter's night with the wind howling and the rain being driven through the roofless ruin. It is said that the ghostly Cunliffe gallops up to the hall, into the building and up the stairs which have long gone and into an upstairs chamber which has also now collapsed. Then comes the screaming of a lady with the 17th century Lord of the Manor finally galloping away into the night. It is said that Lord Cunliffe murdered his wife in that haunted room. The last in the line of the Lords of Wycoller died in the Hall in 1819 propped up on pillows and watching two fighting cocks in mortal combat. No wonder that the Brontë sisters derived so much inspiration from the folklore of Wycoller, but there is also much here to inspire the social historian.

Despite the development of the Country Park, 18th century Wycoller remains an unspoiled example of a handloom weaving village trapped in a time warp which defies the centuries. Some idea of this illustrious past can be seen in the displays within the Information Centre. Here are an assortment

of looms, farm machinery and carts, horse tack, and a display of the history of hill farming.

Strollers through the village should cross the packhorse bridge, turn right between the stream and Wycoller Hall before crossing the water again over an ancient clapper bridge. Between the two is the ancient ford over the river an area featured in the film *The Railway Children*. A short footpath then turns left in front of a garden centre and cafe and follows the stream past picnic tables and between a number of specially landscaped ponds which are popular with breeding frogs and dragonflies. After crossing a wooden footbridge the short track leads past a wooden seat, crosses the stream via a stone bridge and then turns left, back to Wycoller. After passing a picnic site and duck pond on the right pass between the stream and the

Wycoller's clapper bridge in the foreground with the packhorse bridge behind.

Information Centre and Wycoller Hall on the right.

This is bird watching country and along the river there are breeding dipper, kingfisher and grey wagtail. For those who want a slightly longer walk it is possible to turn right along the river at the stone bridge and visit a small waterfall and then retrace their steps to the village. We love this stretch as it provides water deep enough for our black labrador to swim and also fishing pools for the kingfisher especially where alder trees overhang the water and provide excellent hunting perches.

Another fascinating feature of the Wycoller area are what are known as the vaccary walls. In the past some have suggested that they were built in Roman or Saxon times to confine the grazing oxen which worked on the farms. The majority opinion these days, however, suggests that these great stone slab walls were constructed between the early 12th century

Inside the Information Centre at Wycoller there is a collection of old looms and farm machinery.

and the early 15th century. A vaccary was the medieval term for a cattle farm. There are good views of the vaccary walls to the left of the pathway on the way back to the car park, and also feature on other longer walks around the area, details of which can be obtained from the Information Centre.

Barley to Roughlee & Newchurch

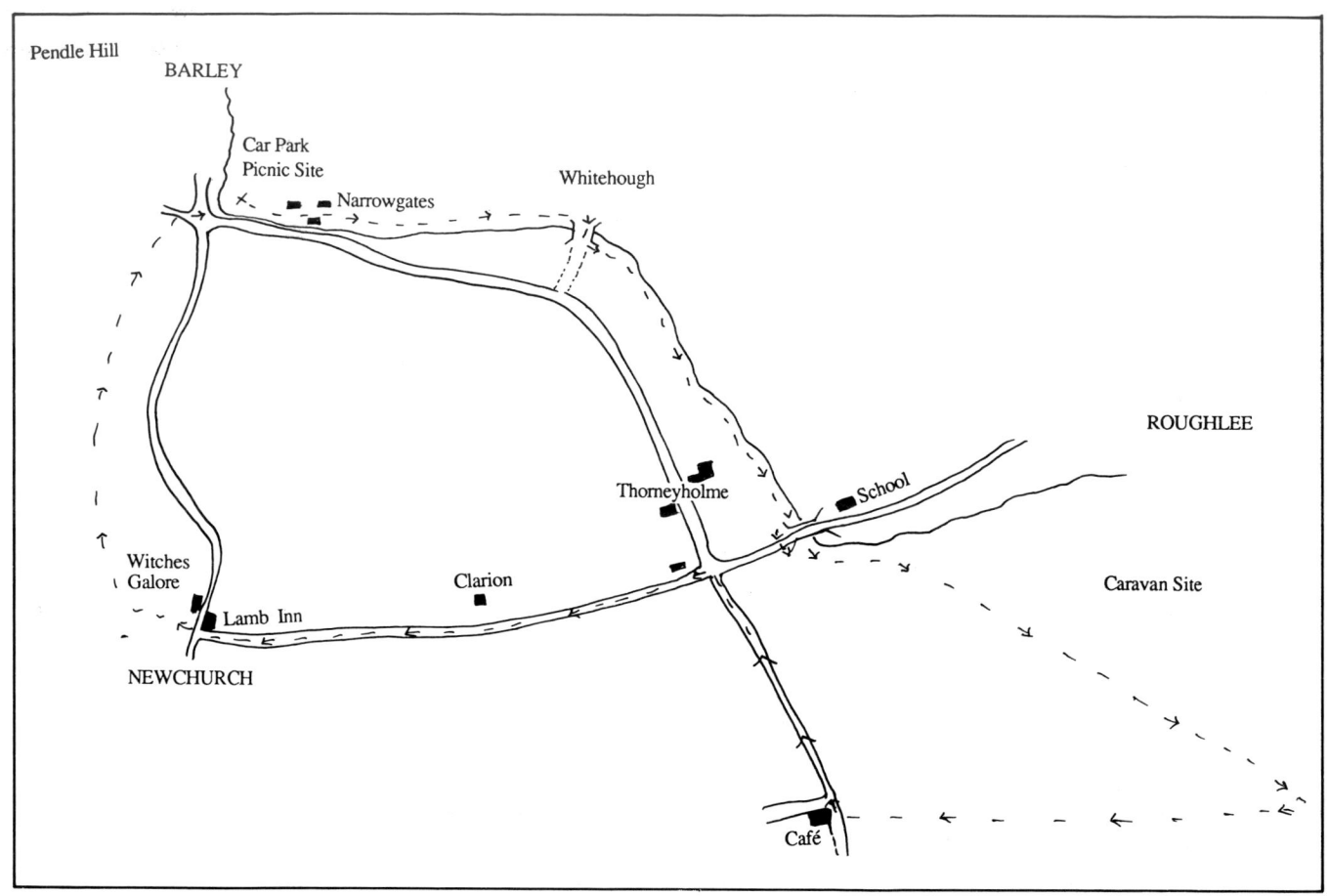

Walk Two
Barley to Roughlee & Newchurch

ACCESS:

From the Padiham bypass, turn left at the village of Fence signed Newchurch. Continue to follow the signs for Newchurch. From Newchurch climb steeply along the road signed Barley. The final mile is a steep descent to Barley. Turn right at the bridge opposite the village hall and find the Picnic site on the left. There are toilets here and an Information Centre.

THE ROUTE:

Begin at the picnic site in Barley. Walk towards the old mill chimney and away from the village. Follow the path between the cottages and then along the river towards Roughlee. Pass a farm and a group of new houses on the left and then pass Whitehough House also on the left. Cross a track and pass through a stile into a damp field. Wellingtons or strong shoes will be needed at this point especially after rain. Follow a path over fields to Thorneyholme Farm and continue along the riverside keeping the water on your left. This meets the Roughlee road close to a bridge. Cross the road and continue along the riverside path. Again this can be quite muddy. The route bears right, climbs through trees and can be difficult to follow. Keep diagonally up the hill, across a number of stiles and join a track running across the hill. Turn right along this track to a small cafe and shop on the corner of the Roughlee to Fence

17

*St. Mary's
Church in
Newchurch*

road. This building was once a toll house for the old road down
into Nelson. Turn right and descend the road to Happy Valley.
At the cross roads turn left and follow the road up to
Newchurch, passing the Clarion Tea Room on the right. In
Newchurch the Lamb Inn serves bar snacks, there is a gift shop
and a toilet block. By the toilet block find a footpath sign
indicating Barley which is reached after one mile of rolling
countryside with magnificent views of Pendle.

OUR WALK:

Allow 3 or 4 hours for the 5 mile round trip.

The three villages linked by this walk are among Pendleside's most delightful settlements and have one thing in common – witchcraft. Despite their beauty, all have seen more than their share of skulduggery in times gone by. Barley, known as Barelegh in 1324 and meaning the infertile meadow, was the home of one John Robinson. He antagonized one Elizabeth Device after fathering her illegitimate child. The seventeenth century was a period of superstitions and the clay models which the so called witch was alleged to have made of him were thought to have brought about his death. Whilst most of the witches were probably cantankerous and frightened old women, Alice Nutter was no such creature. She was well to do and lived at Roughlee Hall. Even so, she was adjudged a witch and

The main street in Newchurch showing Witches Galore

Narrowgates Cottages, once the home of workers at the mill shown in the background, which is now a private house

rounded up with Demdike and the rest. Demdike, otherwise known as Elizabeth Southern, was perhaps the most notorious of the Pendle brood. It was at Newchurch that this old besom first came in contact with the devil. In those days the area was called Goldshaw Booth and since then the New Church of St Mary has been built and the village gradually assumed its name. The church has a splendid tower and if you look over the doorway you will see that an 'eye' has been carved there; this is known as the eye of God. This keeps watch over the village whilst its inhabitants are at prayer. There are many flat gravestones in the churchyard, but these have not always rested in peace. The Kirk gang, a group of cut-throats with a name and reputation as rough and as tough as Jesse James used to hide their loot beneath the flat stones after their regular raids on the outlying farmsteads. It also seems that the Witches of Pendle were not averse to doing a Burke and Hare act, and in the witch trial at Lancaster in 1612 James Device testified that Old Mother Chattox took four teeth and three scalps from the dead in Newchurch.

Before we frighten our readers away from Newchurch in case it goes dark early, let us say that this is a lovely village which has a lot more to offer than crime. In the churchyard the stone sundial is well worth a second glance, the aisle has a unique set of fluted pillars, and the church also owns a lovely silver Stuart Chalice. James Moore an outstanding astronomer, later to be knighted, but no relation of Patrick, lived hereabouts in the 17th century and was for a time a tutor to James II. He was also the surveyor in charge of the draining of the Fens and had much to do with the founding of the Royal Observatory. He must have been alive at the time of Civil Strife in England and may well have found, like those of us who walk these hills today, peace and seclusion which is so lacking in the cities. One visitor who came to the area looking for peace certainly went away disappointed. This was John Wesley who visited Roughlee in 1748 to preach. The Vicar of Colne, the Reverend George White, had other ideas and hired a mob to disrupt the meeting and Wesley was well and truly roughed up.

Whenever we walk this route we can feel peace descend as we follow the old road through Narrowgates cottages, now very tastefully modernised, and reach Pendle Water chuckling its merry way over its pebbly bed. In winter siskins and long tailed tits feed on the seeds of riverside alders, and by February the butterbur is beginning to push up its compact pink flowers. By midsummer the leaves have grown into huge umbrella-like tufts

A delightful country scene between Whitehough and Thorneyholme

which give it one of its old country names of wild rhubarb. Butterbur leaves were used to wrap up butter for sale in local markets before greaseproof paper was invented. In even earlier times a potion was made from the plant and used to treat the Black Death. In Germany it was called Pestilencewort and was also used against the greatest killer of the medieval world. Also adding splendour to the summer hedgerows are wild roses, whilst later on in the summer the rosebay willow herb earns its name

of fireweed because of its scarlet flowers. Rosebay is not a native to Britain but was introduced from North America and spread quickly along railway lines and during the Second World War on to bomb sites. From there it spread along riversides, and its leaves during August and September provide food for the huge caterpillars of the elephant hawk moth.

We were once following this particular walk above Roughlee early on a September morning when we heard a snuffling noise in the hedge, and there among the stems of rosebay was a hedgehog busy cracking open the shells of two huge juicy looking snails. In country districts the hedgehog is still very common despite the fact that so many are killed on the road. They are one of the few British mammals which hibernate, and this process is not as simple as you might imagine. The hedgehog about to hibernate reduces its pulse rate and its blood pressure by over 90%, which could well cause the blood to move so slowly that it clots and causes a thrombosis. The hedgehog,

The hedgehog, one of Pendle's most interesting mammals

however, produces a chemical which thins the blood. If we could discover the formula for this substance we might well have a cure for some forms of heart disease. Master Hedgepig was used in Roman times in a rather grizzly way. The skin was fastened to the shafts of the cart so that horses kept their heads firmly fixed to the front. We had another meeting with a hedgehog during a hot summer's day. A sharp shower of rain was striking the huge leaves of butterbur along the riverside at Thorncyholme and was tumbling over the edge like a miniature waterfall. Beneath this cascade stood a hedgehog on its haunches lapping the water and obviously enjoying the experience of a shower.

A walk through the Pendleside villages, looking at the history and wildlife, always makes us think of the use the women in the old days made of the plants. Did they boil up butterbur to cure the plague? Did they gather yarrow which grows alongside Pendle Water to cure rheumatism? Did they rub selfheal into wounds? Did they use lesser celandine to cure piles? And if they did, did people call them witches? And what if they were witches? On walks like this it is possible to see history in the making.

NOTE: Walkers on Sundays and sometimes in holidays will find a friendly welcome and a cuppa at the Clarion between Roughlee and Newchurch. This is one of only two remaining walking centres funded by the Independent Labour party, and which has been popular since the 1930s.

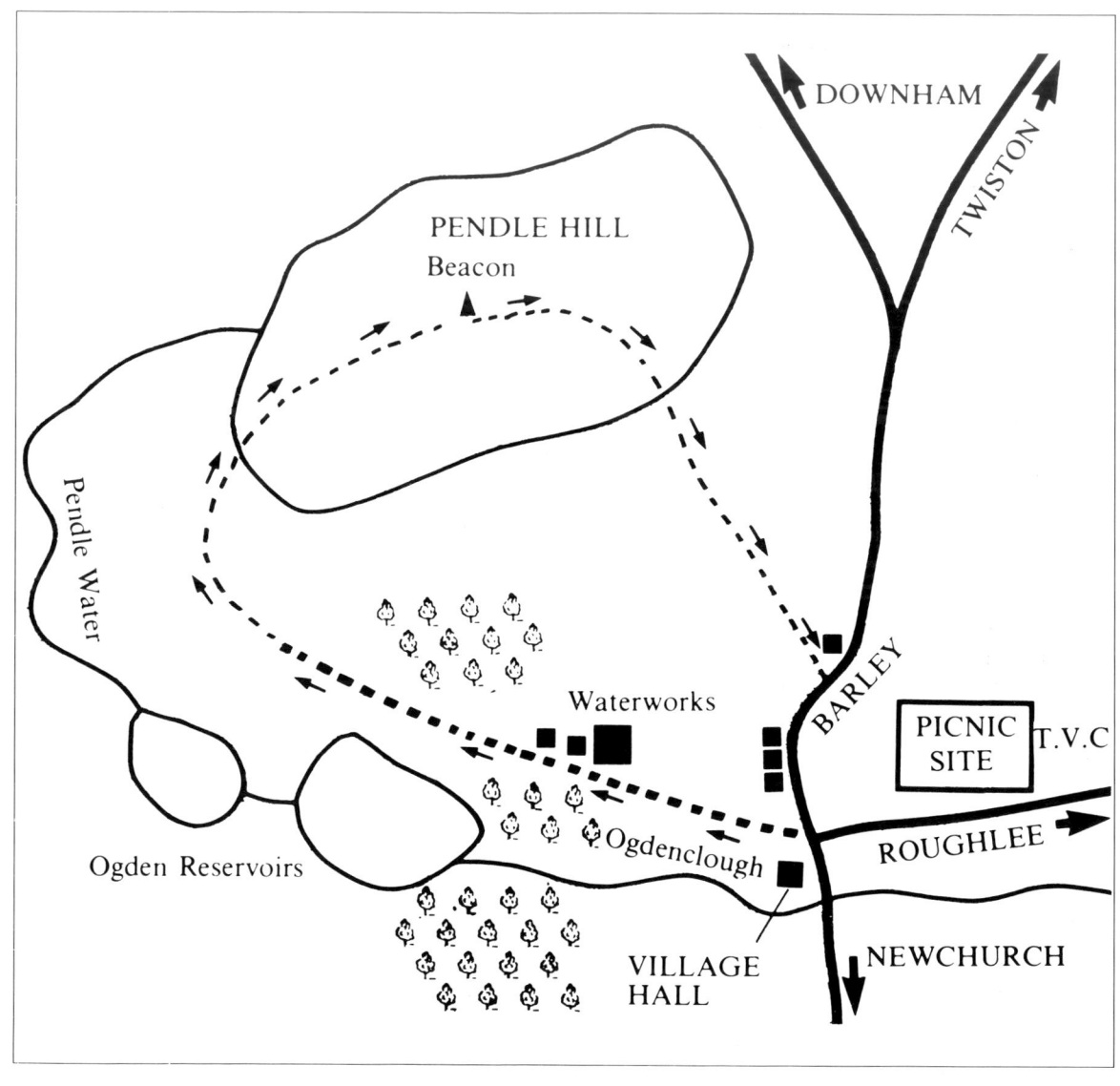

Walk Three
Over Ogden via Pendle

ACCESS:

From the Padiham bypass, turn left at the village of Fence signed Newchurch. Continue to follow the signs for Newchurch. From Newchurch climb steeply along the road signed Barley. The final mile is a steep descent to Barley. Turn right at the bridge opposite the village hall and find the Picnic site on the left. There are toilets here and an Information Centre.

THE ROUTE:

From the picnic site in Barley find the village hall, which is close to the bridge. From the village hall follow the sign indicating Ogden Clough. The waterworks and cottages are passed on the right, and a gentle climb passes a conifer wood and then Lower Ogden reservoir before passing more conifer woodland to the right. At this point the footpath climbs quite steeply, bearing gradually right and leading up to the summit of Pendle. From the flat grassy summit there are splendid views, and the path leading down towards Barley is clearly seen. A stile is found leading towards White Farm House. Turn right through the yard and the path descends through fields and over stiles until Barley village is reached. A right turn at the post office and then left over a wooden footbridge returns the walker to the picnic site and visitors' centre. This is an ideal route for a family and all but the youngest children will manage the trip, but don't let them run downhill!

OUR WALK:

Allow 4 hours to cover the 3 miles. Pendle is an easy hill to climb but this is nevertheless a more strenuous walk than most in this book.

What have 1580, 1669 and 1870 got in common? These are the years when torrential rain caused water to rush like an avenging demon from the slopes of Pendle and devastated many of the villages beneath. We must all wonder if such an event will ever happen again, but the odds must be heavily against this because of the presence of Ogden reservoirs which are fed by many streams and store the excess water and avoid these freak flash floods.

Choose a clear calm day to climb Pendle and as you sit on the summit you can reflect that you are in good company, for in the year 1652 George Fox, the founder of the Quaker movement, climbed Pendle whilst on his way to visit his future wife, Margaret Fell, who lived at Swarthmoor Hall, near Ulverston, in Cumbria. Fox wrote in his diary:
"I was moved by the Lord to go to the top of it, which I did with much ado, for it was very steep and high. When I was come to the top of the hill I saw the sea bordering on Lancashire."

Actually, as hills go, Pendle is neither steep nor high. The walk to the top, if taken slowly, is not too strenuous and the flat summit is some 1,831 feet (nearly 560 metres) above sea level, and so it fails to reach the magic 2,000 feet (609 metres) and be called a mountain. Fox may have exaggerated the toughness of the climb, but he was certainly accurate in his description of the view. Stretching below across the reaches of

opposite:
Pendle viewed from Ogden Reservoir

the valley is the silver ribbon of the Irish Sea, with the coastal complexes of Blackpool and Morecambe laid out like a map. These resorts would, of course, not have been built in the time of Fox, but the valley and rivers as seen today have changed little in the intervening period.

We follow this route several times each year, at all times of the day and at Easter and Halloween at night as well, but we prefer it during spring and early summer. We usually leave Barley just after sunrise and spend some time sitting in the woods of Ogden listening to the owls, and looking for their pellets which are often disgorged as they are at their roosts. Owls swallow their prey whole and any hard parts such as bones and feathers would damage their intestines, and so the sharp and potentially lethal material is ejected in the form of a pellet. Owl pellets are more studied because they are larger and contain bones, but actually all birds, including the robin and the wren, produce some sort of pellet. It is interesting to soak the owl pellets in hot water containing a drop or two of disinfectant and then to pull them apart and so find inside the skulls of the mammals they have been eating. Ogden woods are teeming with bank voles, short-tailed voles and long tailed field mice, and the skulls of these charming little creatures are always found in the pellets of our Ogden owls.

It is not only owls which hunt for these rodents, and as we walked the path by Ogden reservoirs we disturbed a stoat, which shot out of a stone wall in front of us and scampered through a gap in the fencing and headed for the safety of the woods. Its low-slung body and its short legs made it look almost snake-like as it moved. A mallard rose from the edge of the water and quacked its annoyance at being disturbed. For some reason Ogden reservoirs are not popular with birds, perhaps because they are exposed and neither do they contain much food.

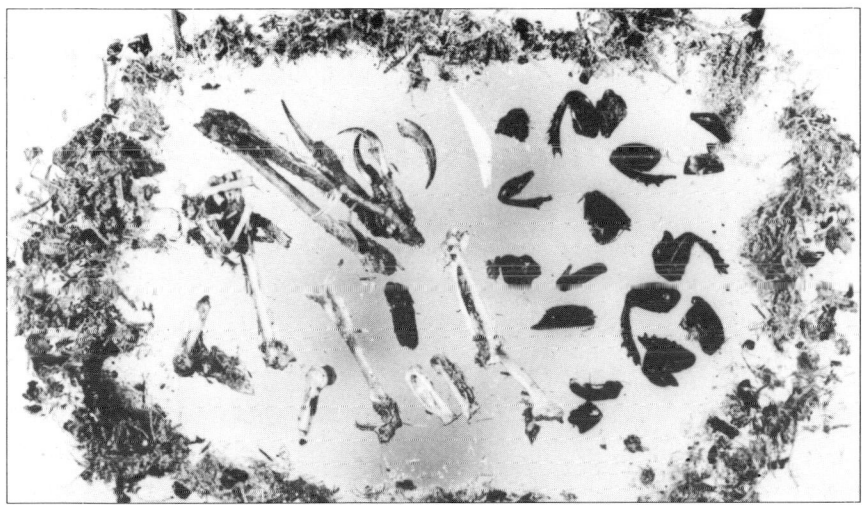

The best time to find wildfowl here is during periods of autumn fogs, when migrating birds, including whooper swans on rare occasions, become disorientated and land until the visibility improves. In the last few years footpaths have been laid out through the woods and provide excellent opportunities for bird watching.

From this point the climb to the summit only takes about half an hour and is followed by quite a number of walkers, especially during the summer. We have lost count of the number of plastic bags we have brought down from these slopes. Not only are they unsightly but they are potentially lethal to sheep and cattle. Its not surprising that some farmers hate hikers, when careless people leave such rubbish and then forget to close his gates! The last few feet to Pendle's summit is quite steep, but the flat bilberry-strewn top is rich in bird life, including wheatears and dotterel, both summer visitors, but meadow pipits, lapwings, golden plovers and even curlews can be seen on all but

The contents of an owl pellet found in the coniferous plantations around Ogden at the foot of Pendle

the coldest of days.

In his book "Rambles by the Ribble", published in 1881, William Dobson included a chapter on "The Botany of Pendle" in which he mentioned that bird's eye primrose grew on the slopes of Pendle, but despite several long searches we have not been able to find it, and must regretfully admit that it has gone for ever. The streamside descent into Barley, however, is colourful in summer with splashes of watercress, water forgetmenot, monkey flower and brook lime. There are some delightful specimens of ash which in winter display their unique black buds, in summer add their own shade of delicate green to the scene, whilst in autumn the ash keys hang gracefully from the branches. Whilst they are still green the keys used to be gathered by the countryfolk, pickled in vinegar and eaten on salads. Farmers also found a use for ash timber. Its wood is so pliable that it does not snap under pressure and was used to fashion axe and hammer handles, shafts for carts, and in the early days of the motor car the chassis was made of ash. Long before the Normans came to these parts the ash tree had its place in mythology, for in the old Norse religion the god Yggdrasil was supposed to live in an ash tree. Keeping watch from the tree top was an eagle, and waiting to pounce down on the roots of hell was a dreadful carnivorous serpent, Niddhogg. We humans lived in the branches and messages were said to be carried by a squirrel who was Yggdrasil's messenger.

All our local trees have a similar folklore and it is no wonder that folks got scared by tales of the witches when the wind howled over Pendle and thunder and lightning filled the air. Man has actually known Pendle's moods for much longer than this, and on the summit there is a Bronze Age burial mound possibly as old as 7,000 years. Appropriately named the Beacon, it was used as a warning fire at least up to the early 19th century. Some folk still carry a stone to the summit each time they make the pilgrimage and add it to the pile. Perhaps in a century or two Pendle may yet become a mountain!

Wheatears arrive on Pendle at the beginning of April and leave in September or October at the end of the breeding season

Barrowford to Roughlee

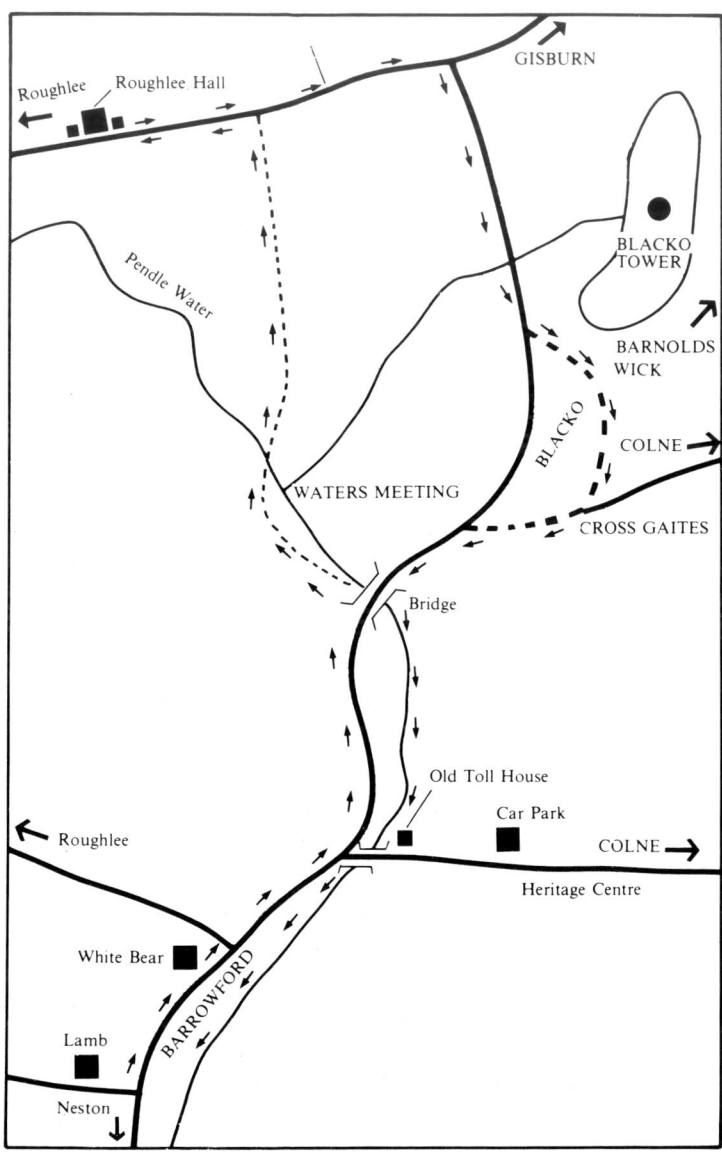

Walk Four

Barrowford to Roughlee

ACCESS:

Barrowford lies astride the A682 road from Nelson to Gisburn. There is parking opposite a garage, close to the White Bear and opposite the Pendle Heritage Centre.

THE ROUTE:

Begin at the Lamb club at Barrowford, which is at the junction of the road to Wheatley Lane. Follow the main road towards Gisburn and pass the White Bear pub on the left. The White Bear serves Bar Snacks. Next pass the road forking right to Colne over a bridge. Note the old Toll House and, if you have time, visit the Pendle Heritage Centre. Some 400 yards onwards, towards Gisburn, a signpost points left at a bridge and indicates the route to the Water Meetings and Roughlee. Follow riverside path past old tennis club and on through several stiles. Pass along narrow lane by ivy-covered cottages. Turn right through stile and over wooden bridge. Turn left and reach the point where two watercourses join. Look up to the right. Cross the wooden bridge. Climb hill through fields to stile. Follow the path which emerges after passing through damp meadows (you will need wellingtons if it has been raining) on to the Blacko to Roughlee road. Spare time to go down into Roughlee and look at the hall where once lived Alice Nutter. Then retrace your steps and follow the main road to Blacko. Bell wood is signed left off this road and well worth a short detour. Blacko Tower dominates the hill. Turn right and descend through Blacko village to Barrowford.

OUR WALK:

Allow at least 4 hours for this round trip, a distance of about 4 miles.

This, like all walks in this book, is enjoyable in any season, but its beginning has strong associations with the May Day of Old England. Those in peril use a May Day call to ask for assistance. Moscow's Red Square on May Day once echoed to the stamp of marching men and clanking weaponry. In times past, however, May Day meant but one thing – summer was acoming and country folk had a good reason to celebrate. We appreciate the sunshine after a hard winter, but how much more pleasure would the first rays of heat give in the old days with no central heating, preserved foods and ease of transport. The Lamb Inn, one of Barrowford's oldest and most attractive buildings had its own May Day "do". Imagine yourself eating a large helping of nettle pudding made to celebrate Nick O' Thungs charity. It was all "American Tom's" idea. If you are a bit confused let us clarify things for you. Tom had returned from America during the reign of Queen Victoria and suggested that an excuse was needed to rivive the revelry of May Day. Nick O'Thung was invented and Tom suggested that members of the Lamb club should celebrate his charity. A walk was to be undertaken from Barrowford to Twiston Moor via the Waters Meetings and Roughlee, and this was to be followed by food and suitable beverage. The food included a good helping of nettle pudding, but this was not as bad as it sounded because it was made from eggs, meat and dripping plus young nettles making

up the vegetable content. In fact nettle had long been used by man. Apart from being edible, nettle was found to have coarse fibres which could be woven into cloth. In 1916 the British War Office had captured German uniforms analysed and found them to be 85 per cent nettle fibre. We wonder if we ever intended to drop caterpillars on the trenches! Nettle was, however, often grown in country districts but it was not easy to cultivate because it requires a rich soil. With all the good fertilisers we now use nettles have become a problem. Once the Barrowford lads had "eten" their nettle pudding they were not allowed anything to drink until they had recited, without faltering, a rhyme which ensured their membership to the clan of Nick O'Thung. This related to the obviously eccentric behaviour of one Thimblerig Thistlethwaite who "thinking to thrive through thick and thin through throwing his three thimbles hither and thither was thwarted and thwacked by thirty three thousand

The old Toll House in Barrowford at the junction of the roads to Colne and Gisburn

thick thorns." We think you will agree that it would be preferable to say this before you drank rather than after. Try it on your friends.

The walk the revellers took ensured views of Pendleside at its best, but before you sample it spare the time to have a good look at the White Bear Inn, one of the oldest buildings in the area, being constructed for the Hargreaves family in 1607. The name of this eventual hostelry was not arrived at by chance. Seventeenth century England was tough and liked its sport to be brutal.

Imagine the building standing in its own grounds close to Pendle Water, the hustle and the bustle, the jugglers and the dancers, the priests and the pickpockets, thee and us and, of course, the poor bear and the howling dogs tearing at its flesh. It could also be that the building was named after The White Bear, a powerful battleship of the period. These facts may help you to visualise this magnificent building in its original context long before the road system developed. Once the Turnpike developed the house was in an ideal position to become a hostelry close to the Old Toll House, and many a weary coachman must have quenched his thirst here.

The waters meetings are as quiet as the main road through Barrowford is busy, and it is here that the kingfisher is often seen, its magnificent plumage flashing like jewels in the sun. Winter is a good time to watch them fish, because their perches on alder trees overlooking pools in the river are not obscured by leaves. A summer walk will always provide the keen botanist with an interesting day, and water mint, kingcup, water forgetmenot, himalayan balsam, barren strawberry, water crowfoot, butterbur, meadowsweet and a host of other fascinating plants can be found with little trouble. Herons feed in the shallows, dippers dip on the stones and grey wagtails wag their

opposite:

Blacko Tower, built by an eccentric grocer named Stansfield

The traditional clog maker depended upon a regular supply of alder wood from which to fashion the blocks for the soles

long tails as they strive to keep their balance as they hop from stone to stone in search of food. Alder trees line the river banks and these splendid trees deserve a mention in both folklore and modern science. When cut, alder wood oozes a red sap and in consequence many of the ancient people refused to cut it because of annoying the demon hiding within who would be certain to avenge himself on those who spilled his blood. Any tree growing with its roots in water, however, must have timber suitable for making fence posts and clogs, and so the desire for 'brass' often proved stronger than the fear of the devil. It still does sometimes doesn't it? Of all our native trees Alder behaves like clover and the pea family. Living in its roots it has millions of bacteria which take in nitrogen which makes up 78% of the air and converts this into nitrates. Such plants can therefore live in the complete absence of nutrients in the soil they have bacteria which makes nutrients for them. In this partnership the bacteria gets shelter inside the roots of the tree and the alder shares the nitrates. This biological marriage is called symbiosis.

On reaching the narrow twisting road all walkers, but especially those with youngsters in tow, should take care to watch the traffic. Roughlee is the starting point for another fascinating walk, but the real reason for the visit on this walk is to see the old home of Alice Nutter. Roughlee Hall is now hemmed in by a modern housing development and is itself divided into three cottages, but its old character remains. It is far better to have an old house like this split up and used rather than abandoned and falling into decay.

The return journey involves a steady climb to Blacko, and the tower which stands on its summit is a landmark for miles around. It was not, however, the home of Old Mother Demdike, perhaps the most notorious of the Pendle Witches; nor was it built as a watchtower and beacon site during the Napoleonic

The grey heron feeds regularly along the streamsides around Barrowford, Blacko and Roughlee

wars. For such an obvious landmark very few people are aware that the origins of Blacko Tower are anything but romantic. The Black Hill (which is what Blacko means) is 1018 feet above sea level (about 330 metres) and it really fascinated a chap called Jonathan Stansfield, a grocer who had "med a bit o' brass." In 1890 he decided that Blacko Hill was not high enough for him to see the whole of Ribblesdale, and he was so narked that he decided to add a few feet. However, like the Tower of Babel before it, the structure fell short by a substantial margin, and remains as another example of man's folly.

The site of Demdike's home, Malkin Tower, is not certain; indeed there is much learned on the subject. Certainly there is a place near Blacko called Malkin Tower Farm, and a heap of stones there said by some to be the remains of Malkin Tower. But all is conjective, and there is as much "evidence" to say that the real Malkin Tower was situated in a field near Newchurch.

On the way down the main road through Blacko to Barrowford it is worthwhile to take a diversion through Beverley, and from the road through this tiny hamlet there are several smashing little footpaths leading up on to Blacko hillside. The Cross Gaites Inn has some history of its own and is sited on the old road which ran from Colne to Blackburn. The original owner, or someone long ago, must have had a good sense of humour, because above the doorway is inscribed "Free Ale Tomorrow." Alas tomorrow never comes and we will all have to buy our own as usual. From the Cross Gaits the road descends steeply into Barrowford and the circle is complete. Every time we arrive home, we brew a cup of tea, sit by our fireside and go over the route, thinking of sparkling kingfishers, dancing and baited bears, battleships, Thimblerig Thistlethwaite, American Tom and Alice Nutter. If the weather has been particularly bad we spare a thought for Old Mother Demdike struggling to her hovel wherever it was and long before grocer Stansfield built his folly.

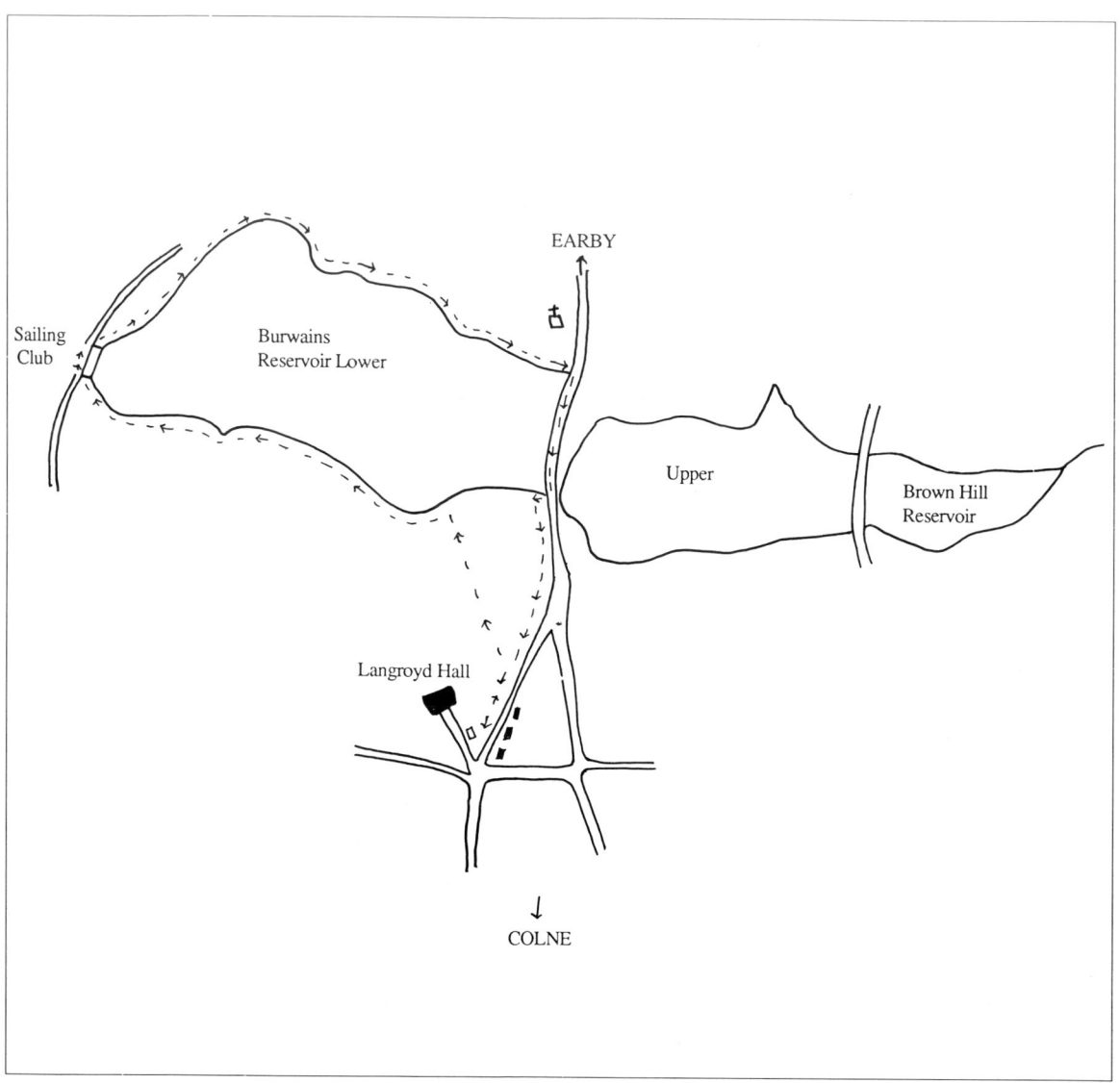

Walk Five
Around Burwains

ACCESS:

From Colne follow the signs for Skipton keeping a sharp look out for the Langroyd Hall Hotel on the left. The hotel serves excellent bar snacks and forms an ideal base for building up your energy levels before enjoying a circular walk around Lake Burwains. For those not eating there is at present roadside parking. Great developments are taking place at the moment and parking will soon be no problem as Foulridge takes its place on the tourist map.

THE ROUTE:

From the Langroyd follow the short minor road towards the Colne Skipton main road, the A56. Pass through a gate in the hedgeside and then strike left across a field to reach the reservoir path. Most of the path has been surfaced with chippings but in wet, windy weather the water can still splash onto the track. Follow the track around to Lake Burwain's Boating Club. At the club gate descend stone steps to the car park and then bear sharp right between the boat club and a group of attractive cottages. The track then continues along the reservoir side with only one point of difficulty. At a finger post resist the temptation to turn left and pass between a group of houses and then onto the Skipton Road. Carry straight along passing the church high to the left and then a bird hide on the

Around Burwains

The coot is a common resident around Foulridge reservoirs

right on a spit of land pushing out into the reservoir. The path continues to the road. Turn right and continue to the garden centre on the left. Turn right off the road onto another well made footpath and return to the car.

OUR WALK:

Here is the perfect walk for those who want to cover a reasonable distance, but do not enjoy climbing steep hills. This is a walk ideal for naturalists and a perfect example of how human enterprises can have a beneficial effect on wildlife. Prior to the cutting of the Leeds to Liverpool canal Foulridge was an area of rolling Pennine moorland and presented a major engineering problem. This is the highest point of the canal and servicing the cut required many locks and at Foulridge itself a

46

one mile tunnel was cut through solid rock. Each time a lock is operated some 75,000 gallons of water is lost and thus Burwains was built to provide the compensation water to keep the canal topped up and running.

Burwains was built in the late 18th century and as it was never meant to provide drinking water, reeds were allowed to grow around the edges and produce a magnificent wildlife habitat. Great crested grebe, dabchick, mallard and reed bunting all breed here and in winter Burwains plays host to both common and rare wildfowl. Smew have been recorded here as have goldeneye, gadwall, whooper swan, water rail and on one March morning we saw a bittern. Throughout the winter a flock of more than 100 Canada geese are present in the area roosting on the water and feeding on the grass in the surrounding fields.

The Langroyd Hall is an ideal hostelry to enjoy a snack before or after the walk around Lake Burwains

This can on occasions annoy farmers as it is estimated that eight geese consume as much grass as one sheep.

With rapid development going on around the reservoir it is fast becoming a popular country park and careful management will be required to satisfy the needs of walkers, anglers, boaters from the Burwains club and especially the wildlife. With care the area will provide for all these needs and few walks are more beautiful than this whatever the time of year but especially on a summer's morning. The colourful sails of the yachts reflect in the water and beyond the sailing club Blacko Tower stands out and behind this the sweeping outline of Pendle. On sunny days the sundial on the front of one of the white painted houses beyond the Boat Club can be seen to be surprisingly accurate.

This is not just a fair weather walk, however, and even in wet and windy weather there are plenty of sheltered areas

A group of charming cottages close to the banks of Lake Burwains. Note the sundial on the wall.

from which there is good birdwatching and especially from the bird hide, which is so popular that there is every chance that others may be added. The hide is certainly an improvement on the days many years ago when the only way to watch birds in this area was to lean over the fence whilst standing on the pavement and being splashed by the traffic on the busy Colne to Skipton Road. Another thoughtful development is the provision of a path to the hide which is suitable for wheelchairs and there is even a space within the hide itself into which the wheel chair can be slotted in front of a window of just the right height.

It was in this area that our good friend the late James Baxter found a dead Manx shearwater in the spring of 1974, a most unusual sighting for an inland area. At this time of year almost anything is likely to turn up on Burwains including black tern, short eared owl, hen harrier, mediterranean gull, ruddy duck – the list is endless and this walk should be on every naturalists' list of exciting places.

For those who just enjoy a quiet stroll close to a pleasant pub then Burwains is still the perfect place.

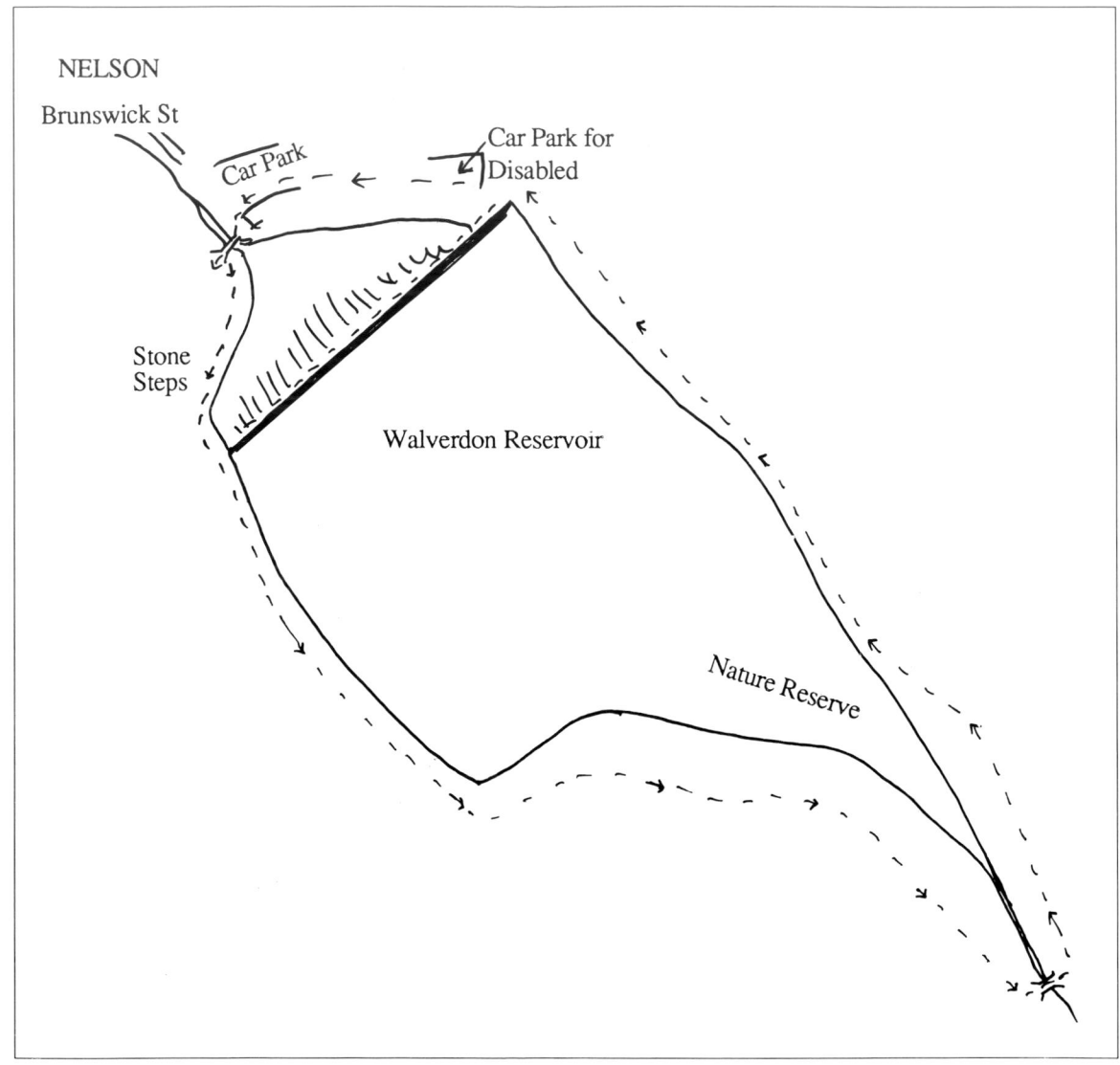

NELSON

Brunswick St

Car Park

Car Park for Disabled

Stone Steps

Walverdon Reservoir

Nature Reserve

Walk Six

Around Walverden

ACCESS:

From Nelson centre find Brunswick Street which is behind the Arndale Centre and the railway station. Proceed up the street until it ends in an area sandwiched between old mills and factories. Have courage and follow a narrow track between the buildings and continue to the extensive car park at the foot of the reservoir.

THE ROUTE:

From the car park cross a sturdy wooden bridge and climb a set of stone steps to reach a choice of stiles at the top. Take the left of these which gives access onto the reservoir embankment. Follow the circular path around the reservoir and return to the car park. This is by no means a strenuous walk, the only climbing being from the wooden bridge onto the embankment. Even this can be avoided as there is a car park for the disabled close to the top of the embankment.

OUR WALK:

One of the most underated strolls around Nelson is the path around Walverden reservoir. The car park is excellent, the short stroll around the water bracing and often full of fascinating birds, especially in winter and early spring, and we can find only one

A pair of mallard staking their claim to a stretch of wall around Walverden reservoir

fault. This is the fact that it is not signed from the town centre.

As we left our car the early morning rain had only just stopped and the excess water was gushing and gurgling over the overflow sluice. The willows were well advanced and the yellow pollenfull catkins seemed to be full of bees feeding greedily on the nectar. This sugary solution is just as essential to a cold bee as petrol is to a motor car. At the top of one of the tallest of the willows a willow warbler sang its heart out as if in defiance of the almost gale force wind which blasted across the surface of the reservoir. From the 15th March to 16th June, Walverden tends to be quiet as this is the closed season for coarse fish. In the fishing season the little jetties provided for anglers are soon claimed often before or just after sunrise. The species caught are roach, tench, bream, perch and carp with tickets to fish obtainable from the warden who is usually on site.

Looking through our nature diaries we find that in June we have seen all three British species of wagtail, the resident pied and grey and the summer visiting yellow wagtail the colours of which are so bright that it rivals even the most attractive canary. In late August we watched brown dragonflies mating, the male and the female flying along attached to each other, a position called 'in tandem'.

Early on a misty September morning we watched three herons fishing on the outlet stream and with the water levels somewhat down following the summer we watched snipe and lapwing feeding on the damp mud whilst overhead swallows and house martins were gathering in large numbers in preparation for their return migration to Africa.

In winter pochard, tufted duck, mallard and coot are always present and in very cold periods rarities such as water rail and hen harrier have been seen. On the same freezing

The spectacular overflow weir leading from Walverden reservoir

January day that we saw the water rail we also recorded jack snipe, dunlin, teal and 12 whooper swans.

Whilst preparing this walk we added to our list of species by spotting a flock of ten goosanders which included nine females with greyish bodies and red heads and only one gloriously white male with a bottlegreen head. Also present were 18 little grebes probably driven to the shelter of the reservoir whilst on a spring migratory movement, and three very hungry looking herons their feathers ruffled by the wind.

Watching the herons and the goosanders it is no wonder that jealous anglers who may have had a bad day get annoyed with these master anglers. We should surely not get too angry because we fish for pleasure whereas the birds fish to stay alive. Only very cruel and selfish sportsmen would begrudge them their fair share.

The stroll should always be taken slowly especially in the warm days of spring and early summer but for those who wish to stretch their legs and walk further then there is an extended route marked to Catlow and Coldwell reservoir and even as far as Wycoller.

In summer both the yellow wagtail (top) and grey wagtail (below) occur around Walverden

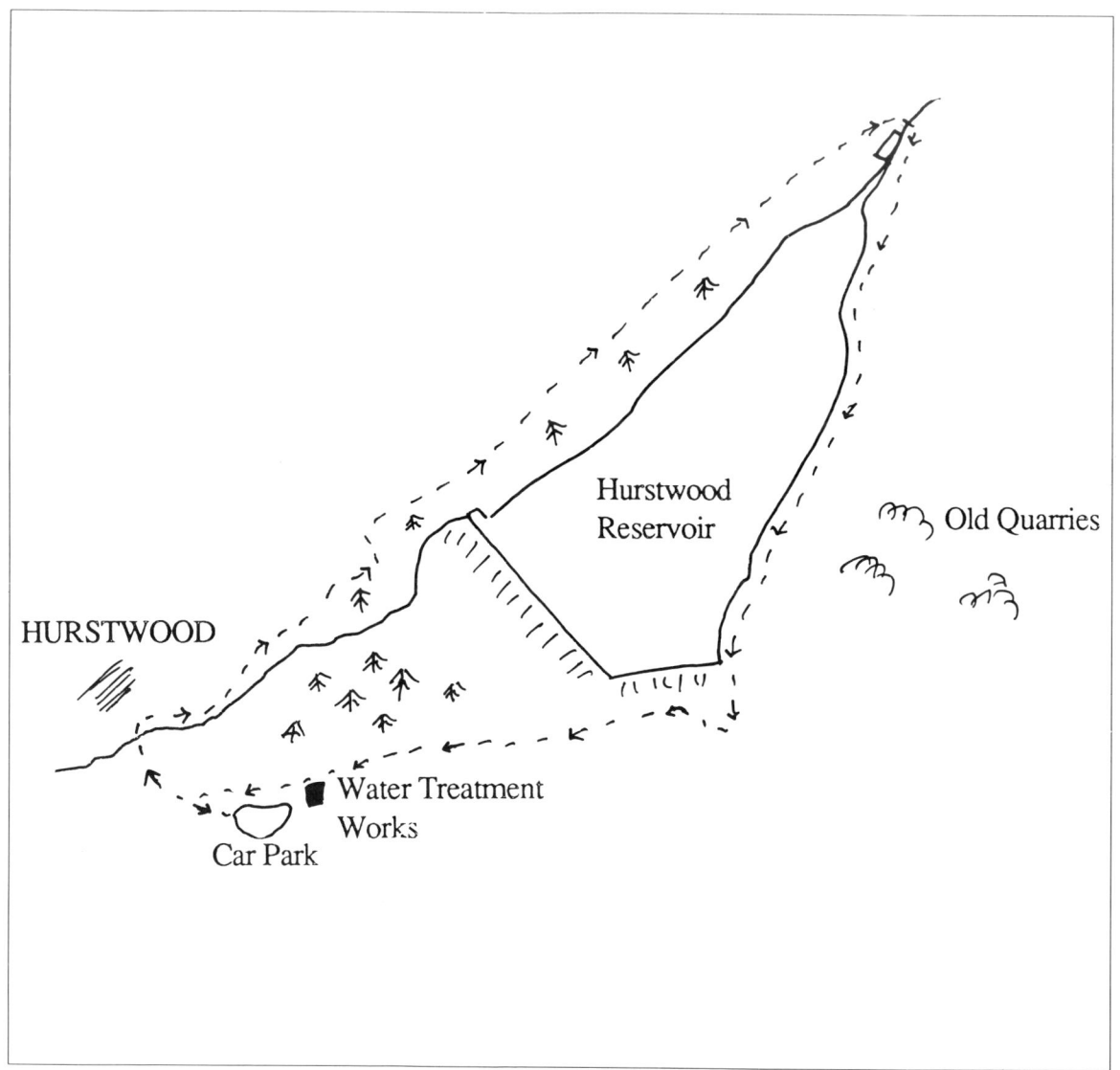

Walk Seven
Around Hurstwood

ACCESS:

Worsthorne is signed from the A671 Burnley to Todmorden Road. Hurstwood is signed to the right off the Worsthorne road and there is a large car park through the village. In Hurstwood itself there is no public house, but the Crooked Billet in Worsthorne provides bar snacks and so does The Kettledrum and the Fighting Cocks on the main Burnley to Todmorden Road.

THE ROUTE:

From the car park head back towards Hurstwood. Turn right and follow an obvious track through a conifer plantation and then around the perimeter of Hurstwood reservoir. Return to the car park passing the water treatment works.

It is also possible to enjoy a second stroll along Cant Clough and through old quarries.

Allow about 3 hours for this 2 mile stroll.

OUR WALK:

Situated in the valley of the River Brun just off the Burnley to Todmorden road, lies the historic little village of Hurstwood. Its history might well go back beyond the year AD 937 when the battle of Brunenburk was fought. It is only fair to point out that other areas of Britain also claim to be the battle ground, but Hurstwood does at least have a "battle stone" down by the riverside. Freeman, the 19th century historian, sets the scene:

"At last the rebellious Danes and their Kinsmen from Ireland who came to their help, together with Constantine of Scotland and Owen of Strathclyde, who did not scruple to league themselves with the heathen barbarians, were all overthrown by Athelstone and his brother Edmund in the glorious fight of Brunenburk. That fight is looked on as the hardest victory that

Spenser House, Hurstwood

Hurstwood Hall, a 16th century building, which has been carefully modernised

the Angles and Saxons ever won."

Serious historians still demand hard evidence for the fight, but it can never now be established with certainty. Whenever we follow the Cant Clough footpath which is also signed from the village we can still imagine the clash of weapons and the agonised screams of the dying. In more peaceful moments dippers bob on the stones, grey wagtails strut gracefully among the pebbles and tree creepers search for insects in the bark of riverside trees. These agile little birds have specially stiffened tail feathers which they use as a prop whilst they feed. Their favourite nest site is behind loose bark of trees such as alder, sycamore and birch. The stroll follows a circular route passing the reservoir and through a conifer plantation where siskin, crossbill and goldcrest can be seen feeding in winter. The descent into the village with its 16th century hall may well have been familiar to Edmund Spenser, author of *The Faerie Queen, The Shepherds Kalender* and other poems which delighted the first Queen Elizabeth.

> And just beside these trickled softly downe
> A gentle streme whose murmuring wave did play
> Amongst the punny stones, and made a sowne
> To lull him fast asleep that by it lay

There is no doubt that Spenser's house, which still stands covered with ivy in Hurstwood, belonged to relatives of the poet, but there is no positive proof that he ever lived there. There is, however, a great deal of indirect evidence to be gleaned from his writings which contain a large number of dialect words known in the north country. This is particularly noticeable in the *Shepherd's Kalender* and, in a letter to Gabriel Harvey, Spenser himself mentioned his use of dialect. He could hardly have picked these up without contact with his northern relatives.

> The gentle shepherd sat beside a spring
> All in the shadow of a bushy brere

This quotation from Spenser could almost have been written in the "Lanky twang" of a modern dialect poet. He seems to have fallen in love with a northern lass – probably Rose Dyneley, a relative of the Towneleys – who preferred another suitor. The spirit of Rose seems to enter into the fabric of the *Faerie Queen* and it may well be that the poet's thoughts frequently returned to the leafy glades of Hurstwood.

Another successful Hurstwood lad was Richard Tattersall, whose name will probably live forever in the world of horses.

Tattersall's Tenement, now usually called his cottage, is situated just beyond Spenser's House and is older than either this or Hurstwood Hall which was built in 1579. Tattersall's is still surrounded by working stables. None of these three buildings are open to the public, although they are easily seen from the village street. Richard Tattersall left Hurstwood as a boy to enter the service of the Duke of Kingston and he must have proved himself very proficient in the handling of horses because in 1766 he was able to raise the money to take a 99 year lease on property in Knightsbridge quite close to Hyde Park. This area would have been much more rural in those days and "Tattersalls" soon became the favourite place for buying and selling horses, a tradition which has held firm ever since.

Tattersall's Cottage at Hurstwood

Hurstwood itself has changed little since Tattersall's day, but some new housing has sprung up on the fringes of the village. The road to Worsthorne meets Saltersford lane, an indication that in the days when salt was heavily taxed the trade route from Cheshire into Yorkshire passed close to Hurstwood, and crossed the river at this point. Another delightful way to approach Hurstwood, however, is across the fields from the old village green at Worsthorne. Butterflies, including the common blue and small tortoishells, feed on nectar from thistles and self-heal which colour the fields with purple and blue a lovely contrast to the yellow of the buttercups. Self-heal was once used to treat wounds, the reason being that the plant recovered quickly from being cut down. It was therefore believed that it had some magical substance which promoted healing. Many old villages which have not been swallowed by towns still have old medicinal plants growing around them. Sneezewort grows in the hedgerows around Hurstwood, and this was used along with yarrow to cure colds. Coltsfoot roots were boiled in sugar to produce coltsfoot rock to treat sore throats. Even daisies, with their clear bright centres, were used to bathe tired eyes.

It is no wonder that Spenser showed such an intimate knowledge of plants in the writing of his *Shepherd's Kalender* if he spent part of his youth in this still idyllic spot. The reservoir which we follow in this walk was built in 1925 but the wildlife is already recovering with wildfowl at home on the water and sparrowhawks and tawny owls breeding in the fringing conifers. It is the perfect blend of ancient village and adaptable wildlife.

Tawny owls breed in the woodlands around many Pennine reservoirs, including Hurstwood

Around Towneley Hall, Burnley

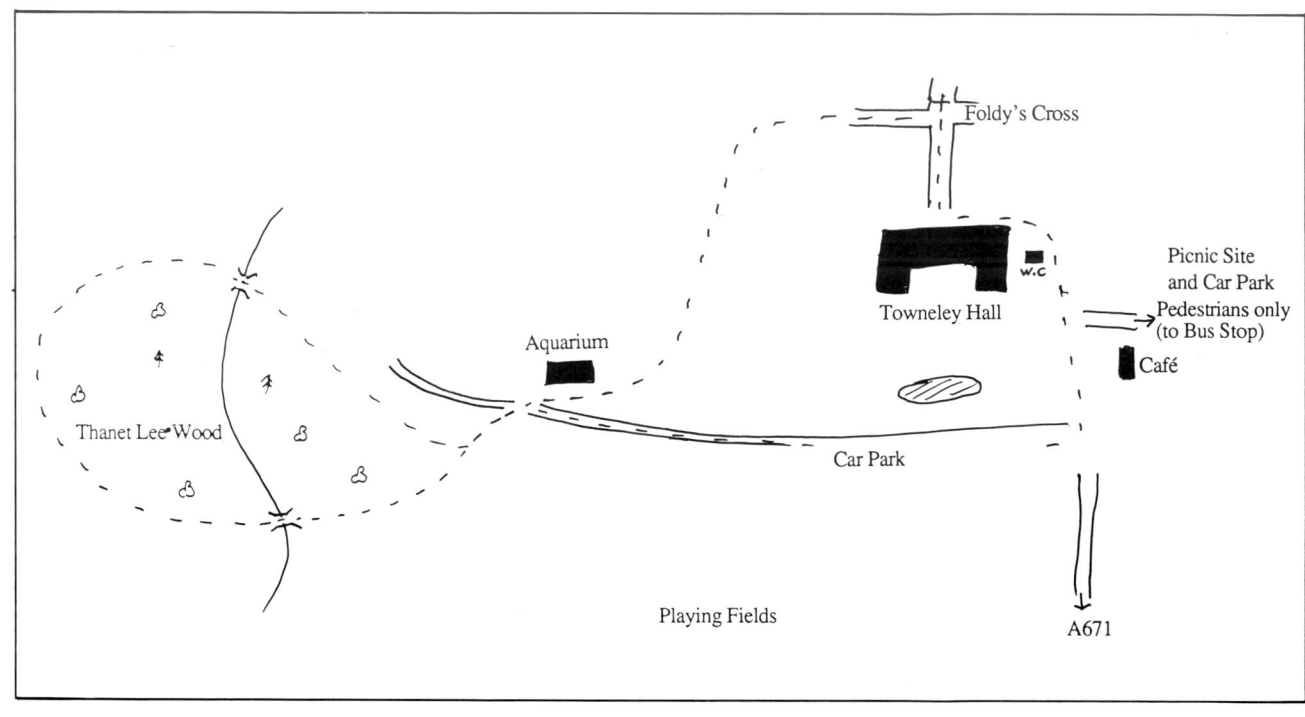

Walk Eight

Around Towneley Hall, Burnley

ACCESS:

Although within walking distance of Burnley Town Centre, Towneley Hall can be reached by car along Todmorden Road the A671. There is parking outside the hall and an extensive car park near the River Calder. For those wishing to have a picnic, first continue along the A671 and follow a second Brown Sign to the picnic site and car park. The number 5 bus marked Towneley terminates at the top gates of the park near the golf course. A gentle stroll downhill leads to the hall. There is a cafe and good toilets.

THE ROUTE:

From the car park at the Hall bear left in front of the hall along the car park itself. Approach Thanet Lee wood. Turn left into the wood and continue around the obvious path. Emerge from the wood and turn right. Turn left into the main grounds of the Hall and follow the track around the nature trail. This bears right and approaches a cross. Turn right and descend the long avenue lined with lime trees to the Hall. Spare time to explore the Hall, entrance to which is free, before returning to the car park. In the season there is a cafe and toilets.

OUR WALK:

Here are 24 acres of woodland walks, marine and freshwater

aquaria, a natural history centre all based on the early 15th century Hall which hosts regular exhibitions, plus the regular displays in the art gallery and the craft and industry museum.

Burnley residents know that all these riches cost absolutely nothing. We had the joy during the 1970s of living in a cottage in the wooded grounds and yet there are still nooks and crannies in the Hall and dells in the woodlands which we once helped to warden that surprise us.

The Hall can be traced back to feudal England of around 1200. The original building with walls six feet thick was built around 1350, but succeeding generations of the Towneley family added to their lands and embellished their house. The men folk were renowned for their exploits in battle and until·the state and church came into conflict the Towneleys were law abiding. From the time of Henry VII, however, the family loyalty to the Catholic faith brought them nothing but trouble. John Towneley (1528-1607) spent 25 years in prison and was only released when he was blind and too old to be considered a threat. Colonel Francis Towneley (1709-1746) fared even worse and was executed for his part in Bonnie Prince Charlie's rebellion. His severed head was kept at the Hall until 1947 when it was laid to rest in the family vault in St Peter's church in Burnley. The political climate was not a healthy one and the Towneleys never achieved high office because of their faith – his was the nation's loss. Surely the bravery of the family could have been put to better use than constructing illicit chapels and priest holes. Probably the best known member of the family made his mark in the arts rather than in politics. This was Charles Towneley (1737-1805) whose collection of classical sculpture was so renowned that the British Museum purchased it after his death and constructed the Towneley Gallery. The family were no doubt delighted in 1828 with the passing of the Catholic Emancipation Act when

Towneley is one of the finest old halls in Lancashire

Peregrine Towneley became High Sherrif of Lancashire, a position also held by his son, Colonel John Towneley. The estate at this time was justly famous for its stock breeding. *Master Butterfly* was a champion bull in 1856 and was sold for a record sum but in 1861 the horse breeders had even more cause for celebration. In this year *Kettledrum* won the Derby at 16-1 and many local folk made a great deal of money. Two local hostelries, the Butterfly and the Kettledrum celebrate these events.

Just when the animal breeding programme reached its peak, the family itself ran out of males. Lieutenant Richard Henry Towneley died only a few months before his father, the brother of Charles Towneley, who himself had only been at Towneley for a matter of weeks. The 40,000 acre estate had to be divided by an Act of Parliament between six co-heiresses and Towneley Hall was given to Lady O'Hagan, Charles's youngest daughter. This generous Lady (1846-1921) finding the Hall something of a financial burden still sold it at a most reasonable price to Burnley Corporation. It opened as an Art Gallery and Museum on 28 May 1903. The family, however, are still intact and influential. Lord O'Hagan is a member of the European Parliament, Simon Towneley who lives close to Towneley at Dyneley is Lord Lieutenant of Lancashire and Peregrine Worsthorne an influential journalist. None of the family, past or present, could have anything but praise for what has happened to their ancestral home since it became one of Burnley's proudest possessions.

We were met by the curator Susan Bourne an enthusiastic and efficient successor to Hubert R. Rigg and Hector Thornton. The latter was instrumental in setting up the Museum of Local Crafts and Industry in April 1971 and he was assisted by the Towneley Hall Society which itself was founded in 1965 and is still going strong. Susan showed us round and we

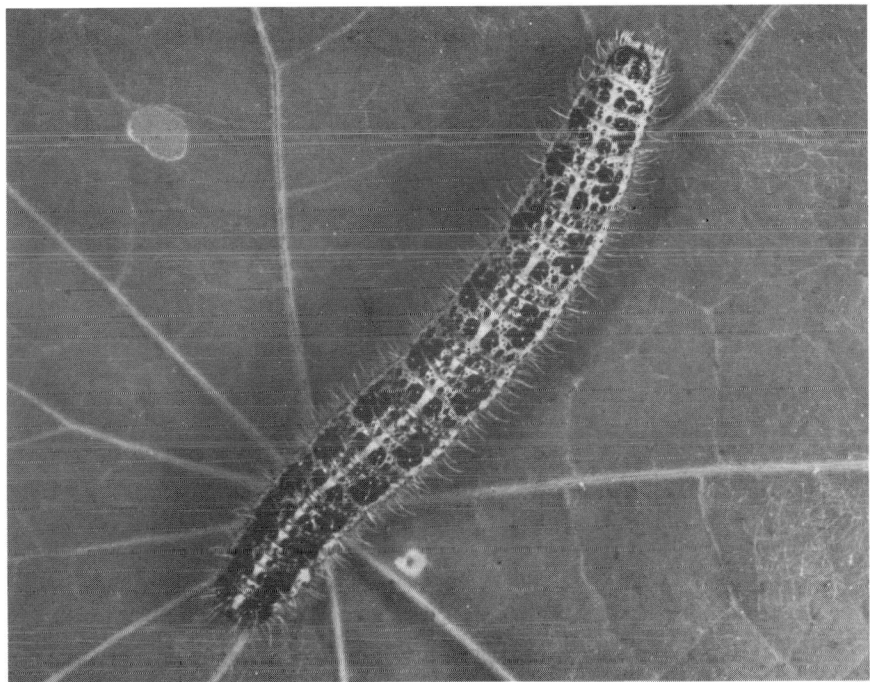

The caterpillar of the Large White butterfly, one of several species breeding in Towneley Park

enjoyed looking at the old pub bar salvaged from the Canal Tavern, a Burco electric washing machine from around 1927, a mock up of a clogger's shop, and a stove used for making oat cakes. Who can remember eating 'stew and hard' on the old Burnley market? We should all jeer at those who demolished much of old Burnley in the 1960s and cheer those who set up the craft museum in the early 1970s and preserved at least some of the history. Our final memory from the museum was of the Lancashire looms and especially the photograph of the knocker-up. The end of a long pole had metal spokes set into it and was scraped against the window of the shift-workers in the days when cotton was king and alarm clocks a thing of the future.

Susan Bourne then took us to meet Dr Mike Graham at the Natural History Centre which is ideally positioned at the junction of two nature trails and stands in some 150 acres of mature woodlands. No praise is too high for what has been achieved here, or for the ambition to improve things still further. Freshwater aquariums show the life in a river from source to sea, and the problems of setting up a marine aquarium have been solved. Plans are afoot to set up tanks to keep octopus and lobsters. These exhibits are sure to delight adults and the school children from all over the county who visit the Natural History

Centre as part of their curriculum. Courses are offered (once again free of charge) on bird watching, pond dipping, plant and tree identification, mammal watching and many others. There is also a developing wild flower garden and an area devoted to British butterflies. Towneley and its friendly staff is all things to all folk of all ages. It offers not one day out but several and whatever the weather there is plenty to do. The gentle stroll through the woodlands reveals flowers in the springtime such as bluebell, wood sorrel and golden saxifrage, summer breeding birds including jay, blackcap, great spotted woodpecker, mistle thrush and dunnock, autumn fungi such as razor strop, sulphur tuft and orange spot whilst in winter flocks of chaffinches and the occasional brambling feed among the beech trees. Along the fringes of the playing fields we have watched flocks of lapwing which are common and twite which are rare birds in Britain.

Towneley Park and Hall is thus literally a walk through history and ideal for any time of the year, but visitors should be aware that the Hall is closed on Saturdays, which is rather a pity.

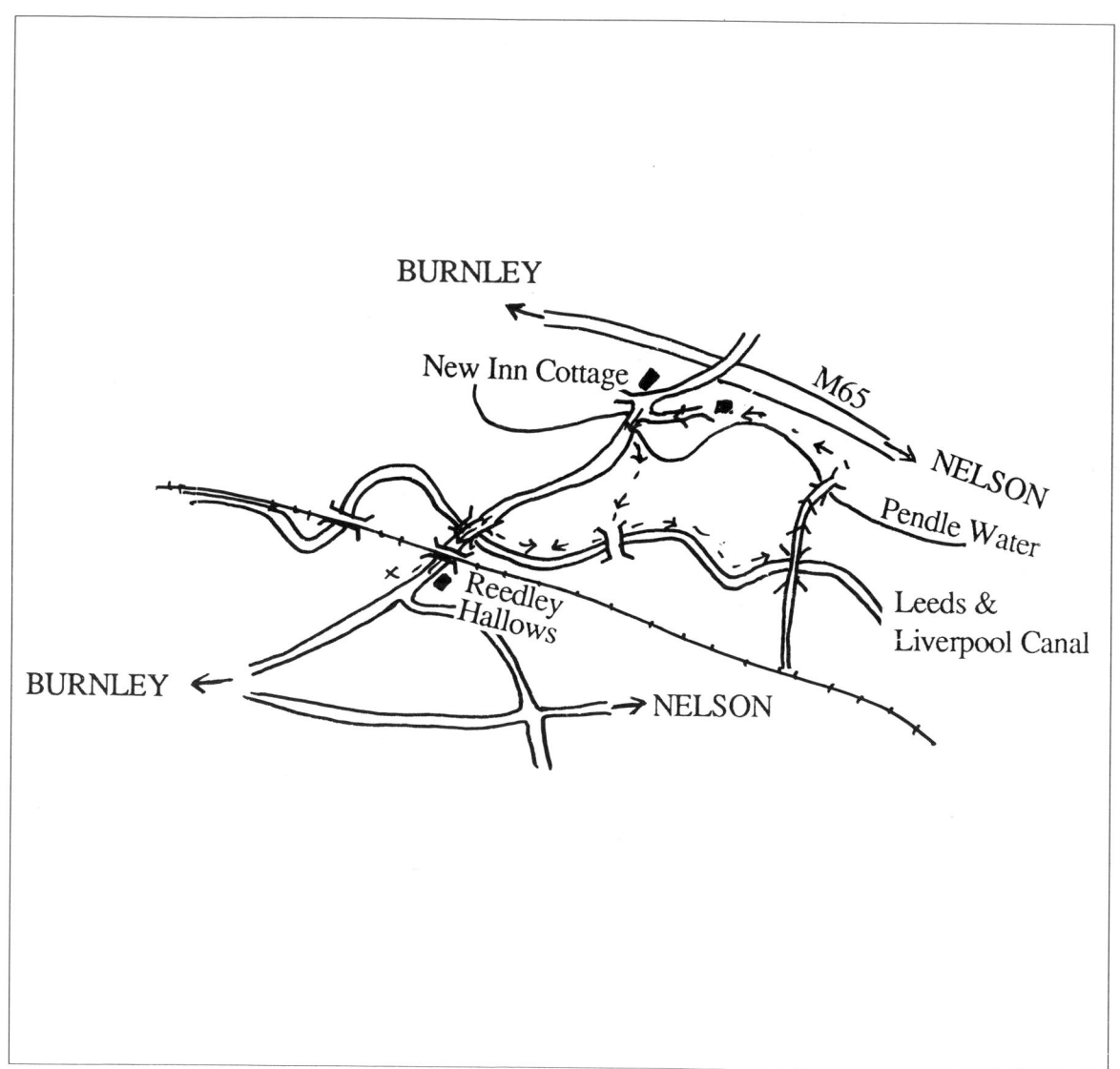

Walk Nine

Barden Lane, Burnley the Canal and River

ACCESS:

From Burnley follow the A56 towards Nelson to a set of traffic lights at Windermere Avenue Playing Fields. Turn left and follow road to a T junction. Turn right and park on the left by a park opposite the Reedley Hallows Hotel. Immediately to the front is a railway bridge. From the Padiham bypass (A6068) Turn right signed Burnley and descend Greenhead Lane. Cross a river bridge and climb a steep winding hill. Pass a housing estate on the right. Cross a canal bridge and pass under the railway bridge to the parking position.

THE ROUTE:

Pass under the railway bridge and Barden Mill on the right. Cross the canal bridge and turn immediately right along the canal towpath. Follow the towpath ignoring a wooden bridge and continue to a stone bridge carrying a track called Robinson Lane over the canal. Turn left and descend to the river. Turn left again onto a track keeping the river on the left. Pass an old farm on the right and continue to the New Inn at Pendle Bridge. What was the New Inn is now a group of cottages. Turn left over the bridge and then almost immediately left through a kissing gate. Ascend along a tree-lined path and then diagonally across a field to the wooden bridge over the canal which was passed on the outward route. Turn right along the canal and

Even in the hard days of winter the canal at Barden Lane is a delightful place to walk

return to the parking position. This walk can be done in around $1\frac{1}{2}$ hours but there is usually so much to see that it is best to allow twice this time to cover the 2 miles of fascinating and varied habitat.

Our Walk:

Of all the strolls in this book, we probably know this one the best as we once lived almost on the banks of the Leeds to Liverpool canal at Barden. It was our regular evening stroll and every inch of it was known to two generations of our black labradors. We have walked here with the canal frozen solid and covered by a layer of thick snow and we have dipped nets into the water warmed by spring sunshine. The presence in the water of large numbers of dragonfly larvae and water lice known to scientists as Asellus always tells us that the canal is reasonably clean and free from dangerous pollutants. We have exchanged friendly words with fishermen in all seasons and with holiday makers navigating long boats along the canal. In the spring we have gathered elder blossom and returned in the autumn to gather juicy berries. The blossom makes a fizzy elderflower champagne and the fruit a rich red wine not unlike port. In the days before the Trades Description Acts it was quite usual for unscrupulous dealers to mix port and elderberry to increase their profits.

The descent to the river is gentle and Pendle Water itself is much cleaner these days. In the days when cotton was king, many mills polluted the water and the long disused Jewel Mill

Asellus, the water louse can withstand moderate pollution, but is killed by many industrial pollutants. Its presence in both the canal and the river mean that both are now fairly clean.

was actually on the line of this walk. So was what the locals have for generations referred to as Jack Moore's Monkey. Every Easter almost the whole of Burnley walked down Barden Lane, over the canal and down to the New Inn on Pendle Bridge. Here were hundreds of stalls, a set of swing boats, pony and trap rides, were on offer and there was a cafe run by Jack Moore and his famous monkey – alas all this has gone but our memories still come flooding back as we reach this section of the walk. These days the river is more peaceful and the breeding area for pied wagtail, reed bunting and the busy moorhens. We found a nest sited among the tangle of alder, willow, reed and yellow flag. The adults have two outer tail feathers which when they are alarmed are waved around like flags. We often wondered what function these feathers served until we watched a family of youngsters follow their parents into the dimly lit but safe area beneath overhanging trees. The young moorhens were very obviously following the white flags of their parents who led them to safety.

The last section of this stroll ascends through damp fields in which breed curlew and lapwing whilst in the drier areas skylark and common partridge site their nests. Even when we lived in the area we were always being surprised by new sightings and never failed to appreciate the beauty so close to the centre of a once very industrialised town. This is true of all Lancashire's towns – they are surrounded by rich and fascinating countryside.

The moorhen is a common breeder in the damp areas between the Leeds to Liverpool Canal at Barden Lane and Pendle Water

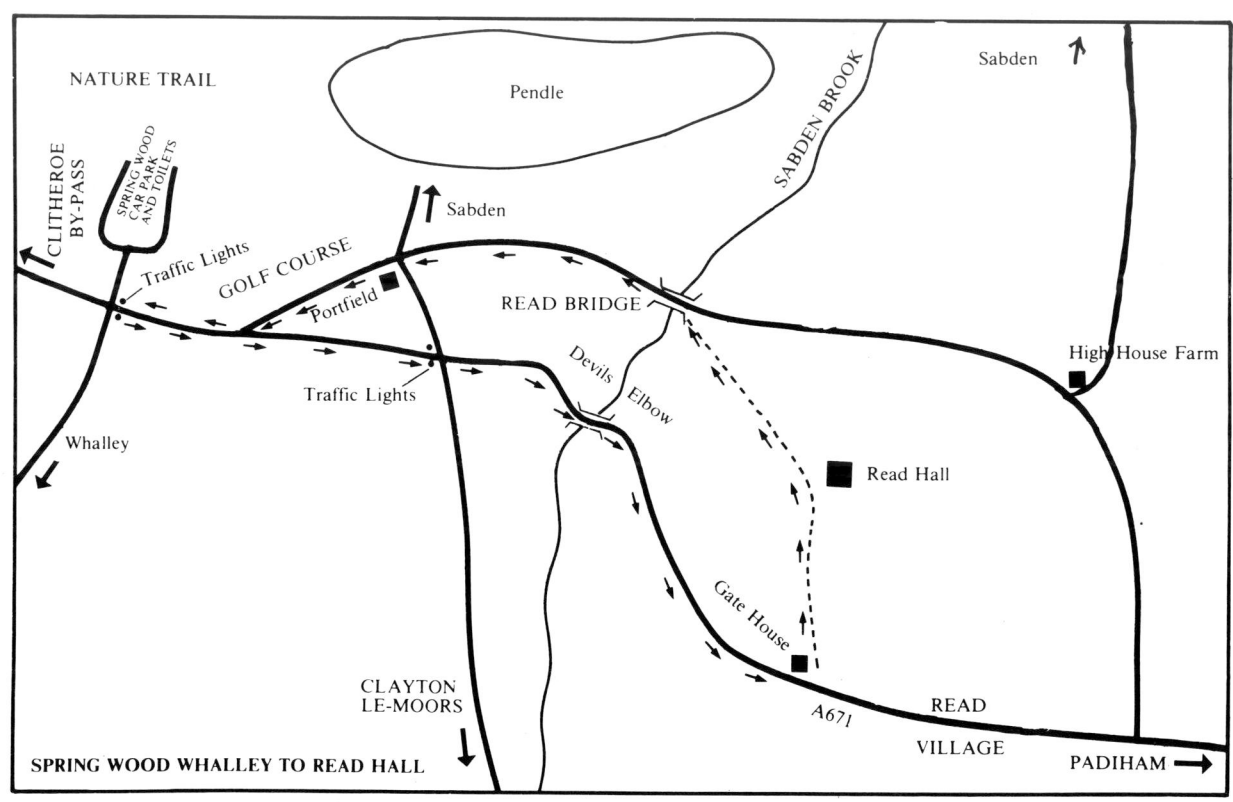

SPRING WOOD WHALLEY TO READ HALL

Walk Ten

Spring Wood Whalley to Read Hall

ACCESS:

Spring Wood is situated above Whalley off the A671 close to a set of traffic lights. Nearby the A671 joins the A59 Clitheroe bypass. There is plenty of parking at Spring Wood and also a picnic area and toilets. It can also be reached from Whalley along a very pleasant footpath, which passes under the A671.

ROUTE:

Park at Spring wood and spend some time following the well laid out nature trails. Then leave via the A671, passing Whalley Golf course on your left. Ignore the left turn to Sabden. Beware of traffic on the busy road but the walk is worth it. Just spend some time looking into the woodlands to the right and left of the road (there is no right of entry). At the traffic lights follow the A671 to Burnley. On the corner is the old Toll house, once a vital part of the turnpike system. Pass Devil's Elbow but look over the bridge at the magnificent Sabden Brook which has carved out an impressive valley for itself on its way to join the Calder and thence to the Ribble. The road climbs and twists and then on the left you will come to the gatehouse of Read Hall. Follow the main drive to the hall until it forks right. The footpath goes left through a farm complex. Good views of the hall to the right and magnificent sights of Pendleside to the front. After the farm the route leads left across a meadow and joins

Bono, our black labrador ready to begin the walk at Spring Wood

the old Read to Whalley road. Turn left and follow the signs to Whalley via Read Bridge and the starting point at Spring Wood. **Precautions**: Several signs during this pleasant stroll indicate that you are following a public footpath through the grounds of the Old Hall and associated farms. Walkers should stick to the marked footpaths from which there are excellent views and keep their dogs on leads, for this is sheep country and a frightened ewe means a dead lamb.

OUR WALK:

Allow 4 hours for this walk, which is just over 3 miles.
Without doubt Read is an ancient settlement. Its origins could have been as follows. Revecht was the ancient name which then

became Reved, which may well have meant Riverhead relating to the nearby Calder or perhaps even to Sabden Brook. By the 14th century the township was dominated by the Cloughs who obtained the ground from the De Lacys. The Nowells took over from the Cloughs and what a family they were! Roger Nowell is perhaps the best known since it was he who played such an important hand in the events which resulted in the deaths of the Lancashire Witches. His story has been dealt with in fact by Bennet in his "History of Burnley" and in fiction, first by Harrison Ainsworth in "The Lancashire Witches". Whilst we find Roger Nowell interesting, we find ourselves more drawn towards Alexander Nowell who was born around 1507 and died at the age of 95. Roger was an important man in local affairs but Alexander was involved in great and dangerous dealings at a national level. His portrait hangs in Brasenose College, Oxford, a sure sign of

Alexander Nowell who died in 1601 at the age of 95

the importance of a man who rose to become Dean of St. Pauls in London. He lived and worked under four of the Tudor monarchs, namely Henry VIII (1509-1547), Edward VI (1547-1553), Mary (1553-1558) and Elizabeth (1558-1603). The Tudor years were difficult times for Church men to thrive. Henry destroyed the power of the Catholic monasteries, Bloody Mary was a fierce Catholic and persecuted Protestants with gusto, and Elizabeth later replied by destroying Catholics. How could a cleric keep his head on his shoulders and die in his bed with his boots off? Alexander Nowell, it seems, had the answer. In the words of the song he had "Gone fishin". The Brasenose portrait of the Dean shows him carrying rod, line and hooks. He is also reputed to be the inventor of bottled beer. Apparently he had taken a picnic with him and placed his ale in the river to cool. He was then called away and forgot the ale until he was fishing in the same place some days later. It had built up quite a head and bottled ale was born! Perhaps it was this which kept him healthy.

But did Read have much history before the Nowells? Without doubt it did and in 1948 the Vicar of Whalley, Gilbert Greatorex, published a booklet called "Historical Essays on Read-in-Whalley", and in it he wrote that "From Cobcar to Padiham heights there runs a stretch of prehistoric road which may well be some 5,000 years old."

Doubtless Read was on an old trading route but modern research disputes its claim to date back to the Bronze Age, but it was quite probably important in Saxon times. As you reach Read Bridge from the lovely green field you are standing on history which, although more recent, is well documented and brutal enough to make the blood run cold. It is difficult for us to imagine what folk must have felt during the Civil War of the 1640s. It often set father against son, brother against brother and

Read Hall with its fine Georgian facade

man against wife. Much blood was spilled and fortunes changed hands at the drop of an axe. The local families took sides and feelings ran high. For the King we had the Towneleys of Burnley, the Nowells of Read, the Talbots of Dinckley, the Shireburns of Stonyhurst and the Parkers of Browsholme. For Parliament there was an equally impressive array including the Shuttleworths of Gawthorpe, the Bradylls of Portfield, the Starkies of Huntroyd and the Asshetons of Downham.

It does not seem to be too much of an exaggeration to suggest that the battle, if such it can be called, which took place at midday on Thursday 20th April, 1643, could well have turned

the course of the Civil War in Lancashire. A strong Royalist army of about 4,000 men was directed into these parts to remove a large supply of arms being held at Whalley Abbey. These men, led by the Earl of Derby and his Lieutenant, Colonel Tildesley, were also told to scatter the numerically inferior force of Parliamentarians. After an unsuccessful skirmish at Whalley, the Cromwellians retired towards Padiham and were followed by the King's Men who had to cross Read Bridge (the A671 did not exist at this time). The Royalists hot in pursuit of, and by now heavily outnumbering the enemy, were ambushed at Read Bridge and suffered such heavy casualties that they were never again a force to be reckoned with in this area.

We walk this route many times a year, but we always try to do it on or around the 20th April, when the chiff-chaff can often be heard calling from the woodlands and the banks are dotted yellow with primroses. In rain the old bridge often looks severe but bathed in sunlight, whatever the season, it looks splendid as the gurgling water rushes under its high arches. Grey wagtails flirt with the swirling water and turn over pebbles in search of stone fly larvae which are common in Sabden Brook. Last spring we sat by the bridge day-dreaming and wondering if the dead from the battle of Read were taken sadly home for burial or removed to a communal grave at nearby Hammondsfield as tradition maintains. Suddenly we were brought down to earth by the rich rippling song of the curlew as the male lay claim to his breeding territory. He then held himself in the air as if held on an invisible wire and then glided smoothly downwards "bubbling" as he went. Curlews often return to the same breeding site and so we returned to our dream world and wondered if distant relatives of this curlew had bubbled over the head of the fishing priest of Read Hall and gone unheeded by the dead and dying around the bridge at midday on April 20, 1643.

Read Bridge, close to which a civil war battle was fought

85

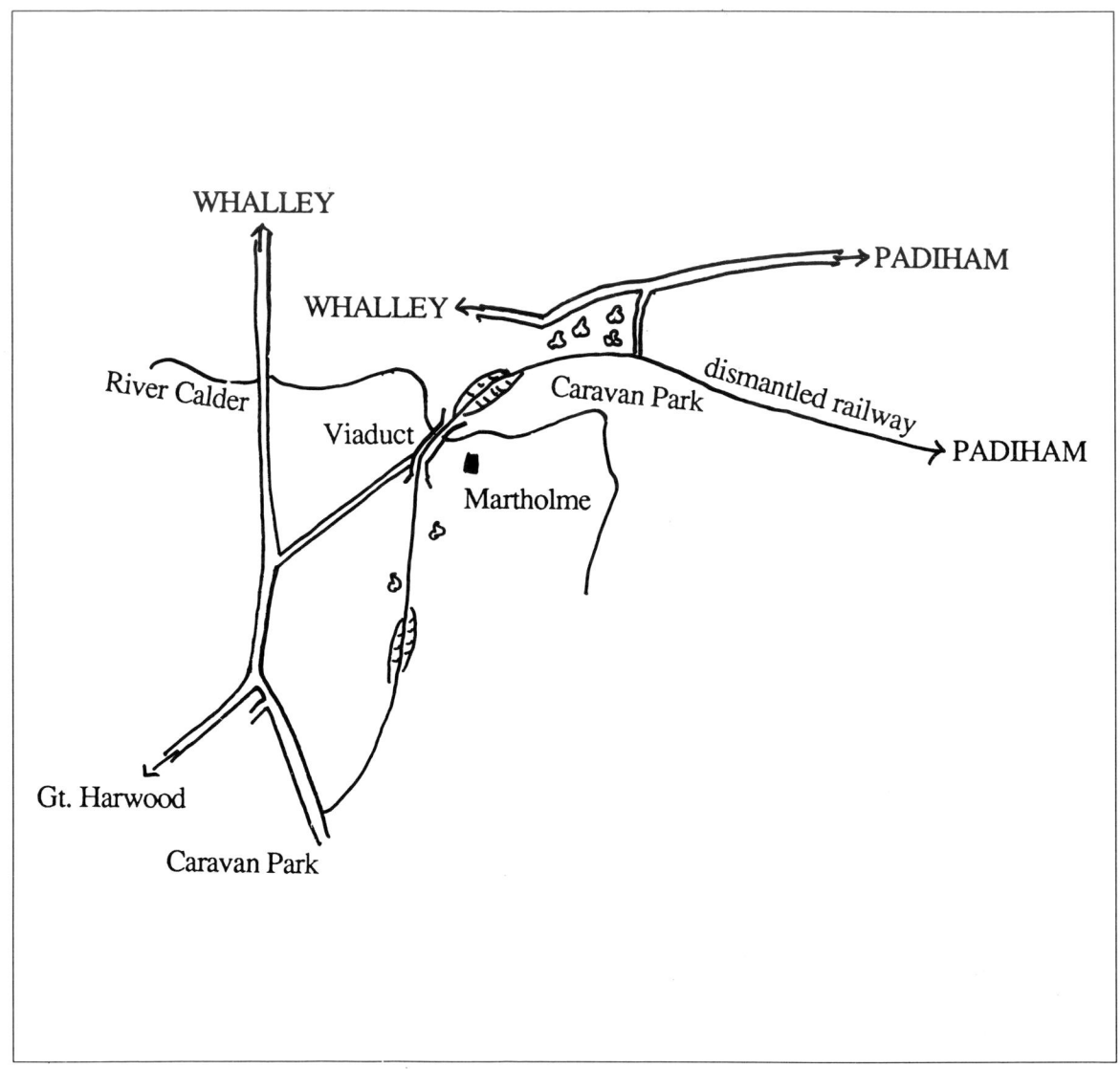

Walk Eleven
On the Great Harwood Loop

ACCESS:

Approach along the Great Harwood to Whalley Road. Just before the Gamecock Inn there is an Italian restaurant on the right. Turn right in front of this and descend towards Martholme. There is parking beneath a railway viaduct which is a listed monument.

THE ROUTE:

As we follow the line of a disused railway the route is linear and therefore a detailed route is not necessary. Those who enjoy linear walks should first walk towards Read and then return to the car for lunch. The next session can then be spent walking the track to Great Harwood and back.

OUR WALK:

In the 1980s and 1990s it has been good to see the British Countryside protected as a result of public funding. A good example of this is the Great Harwood Loop Line which once connected Blackburn, Great Harwood, Padiham and Rosegrove. It opened in 1877 and closed to passengers in 1957.

As we climbed the solid steps from the foot of the viaduct to the old track the weather, which had been dull all day brightened a little and the views of the Calder Valley spread out like a map in front of us. We turned left over the grassy top of the viaduct at the end of which we had to climb down onto the muddy track. Immediately ahead are fine views of Read Hall described in Walk No. 10. This walk continues and would eventually join the Whalley to Burnley road close to the entrance of Read Hall but we turn round after spending time in a delightful wood to the left of the track. In mid-May this is one of the best bluebell woods we know. Early in June we disturbed a

Martholme Hall has now been splendidly restored as a private residence. Walkers should respect this privacy.

The view of the Calder Valley from the Murtholme viaduct

female woodcock who proved reluctant to fly. We discovered why when with a flurry of feathers four chicks ran like clockwork figures in front of us and sought cover under a tangle of brambles.

The woodcock has a long probing bill ideally shaped for pushing deeply into soft ground in search of worms, insect larvae and other invertebrates. Like the pheasant, this wading bird is also highly prized by sportsmen, who enjoy trying to hit a woodland bird which roosts by day, but when flushed twists and turns along the woodland rides and between the trees, providing a very tricky target. It is very good to eat and a thorough knowledge of its habits during the Middle Ages enabled bird catchers to keep up with the demands from the kitchens. At dusk the birds (probably both sexes) tend to fly along recognised routes to preferred feeding areas, and during the breeding season patrol around their woodland territories with a slow and measured wing-beat uttering an unforgettable call consisting of three grunts followed by a higher pitched 'tis-ic'. This is called 'roding' and it follows a definite and predictable route. Special nets called cockshuts were stretched between trees and across rides, and the fact that this practice was one widespread can be seen by reference to place-names such as Cockshoot, Cockleys, Cockroad and Cock-lea. Doubtless the woodcock was more common when our woodlands were more extensive but our breeding population of about 50,000 pairs is greatly swelled by a winter influx of continental birds which find Britain's oceanic climate mild enough to provide sufficient feeding stations in all but the most severe of winters. The position of the large eyes at the sides of the head means that the feeding bird is able to see to the sides and even behind it, giving the woodcock advance warning of the approach of predators.

The return stroll from the bluebell wood reveals splendid views of the viaduct and beneath it Martholme Hall and farm. At one time this complex rivalled Read Hall in importance. In the Middle Ages there was an important market here but by the 1970s the hall had fallen into a sad state of repair. Happily the building has been restored and is now a most impressive residence.

The Martholme viaduct which is now a listed building spanning the beautiful valley of the Calder river.

After our lunch we set off along the track towards Great Harwood. In contrast to the Read side of the viaduct this path has been surfaced with chippings to produce a delightfully easy walk. It will get better as the sensible landscaping matures and trees such as oak, hazel and ash take over from pioneer species

The Gamecock Inn, one of the best inns and restaurants in the area

such as hawthorn and birch. As we walked we made a list of the birds seen, including magpie, tawny owl, jay, sparrowhawk, goldfinch, greenfinch and great spotted woodpecker.

In the course of writing this book we have covered some walks which are under threat from developers and which need to be watched carefully if they are not to deteriorate. In contrast here is a stroll which is bound to improve steadily over the next few years as the careful planning and landscaping brings the reward of ever more exciting scenery and birdwatching. For those who combine walking with bar snacks and good beer, the Gamecock Inn is a welcome spot. It was once a popular haunt of the Clitheroe-based colliers who worked at Martholme mines, now long closed. The Inn began life as three cottages which were converted to accommodate both the Inn and space for 16 horses. It was once an important coach stop on the turnpike between Clitheroe and Great Harwood. Inside the Gamecock you can enjoy a meal whilst looking at the iron poles, called boskins, which were once used to separate the horse stalls.

The area around the Gamecock and the Great Harwood Loop Line is more attractive in the 1990s than it has been for more than a century. Long may this improvement continue.

The woodcock breeds in the bluebell wood close to Martholme

Along Limey Water, Crawshawbooth

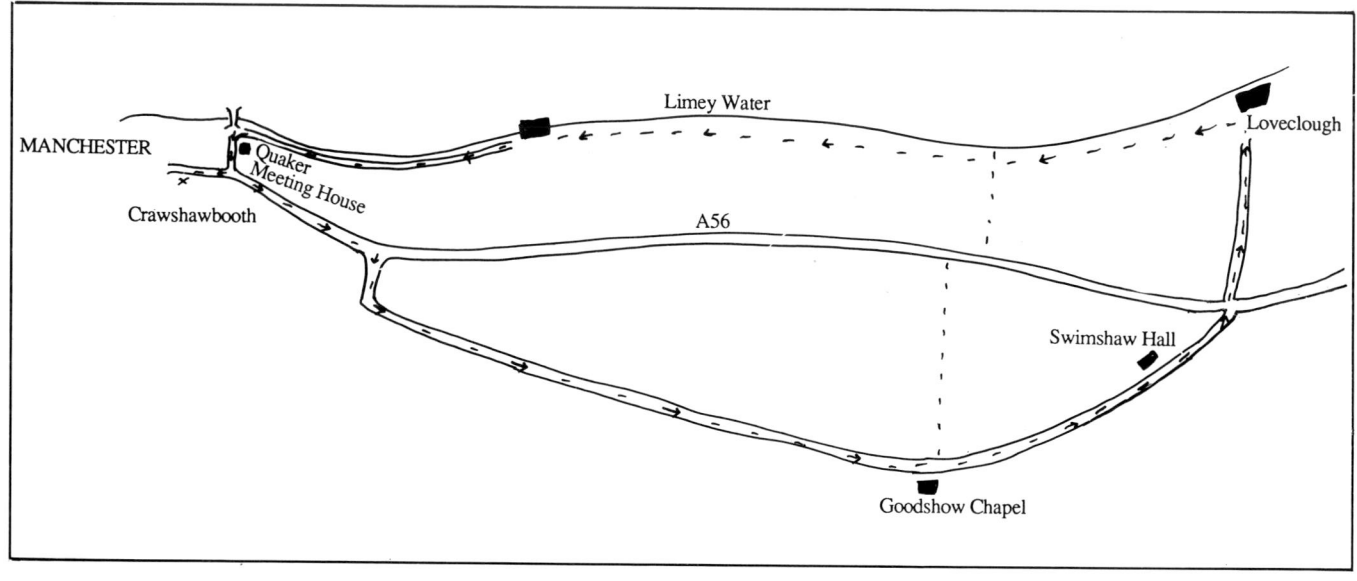

Walk Twelve
Along Limey Water, Crawshawbooth

ACCESS
Crawshawbooth stands astride the A56 between Manchester and Burnley. In the village there is no large car park but several small parking areas.

ROUTE:
From the village centre, climb one of several steep streets before turning left onto a road which passes Goodshaw Chapel on the right. Continue along the winding road which descends past Swinshaw Hall on the left before meeting the A56. Cross this road and descend past a complex of old mills to meet Limey Water. Turn left along the wide track and continue to an old packhorse bridge over the stream. Turn left and pass the old Quaker Meeting House down in a dip to the left. Follow the gently inclined street back into the centre of Crawshawbooth. From the broad tracks followed here there are a number of quiet footpaths which provide ideal places for picnics and links with the main route described.

OUR WALK:
"The huntsmen cheered on the hounds that first hit the scent, loudly yelling loud words, which brought the other hounds swiftly to the Place. These look up the scent, twenty couples at once raising such a babble and clamour that the rocks rang with it.

The hunters encouraged them with horn and voice . . . There was a rocky knoll beside the marsh with a clitter of scree at its foot and out of this jumble of rocks they pushed their quarry, and the men after them. They surrounded the carr and the knoll for they knew by the voice of the blood hounds that the boar was there."

This quote is a translation from a 14th century work called "Sir Gawain and the Green Knight". It tells the tale of the pursuit and killing of the last wild boar in England. There is some argument which can never really be resolved regarding where this event took place. Some favour Widlboarclough on the Derbyshire-Lancashire border, but some dialect experts think that the hunt set out from Swinshaw Hall, in Crawshawbooth. A

Goodshaw Chapel above Crawshawbooth, now happily restored.

substantial hall now privately owned still exists on the site and is one of three reasons why Crawshawbooth ought to be more of a tourists' stopping point than it is. The problem faced by the village is that its modern industrialised portion straddles the main A56 Burnley to Manchester road, but there are fascinating historical areas on both sides of the road. Two of these sites, one being Swinshaw Hall, can be reached by following Goodshaw Avenue up a fairly steep hill to Goodshaw Chapel. A baptist chapel has been on this site since 1685, but the present building only dates from 1760. It is a very early example of a non-conformist chapel in the days when religious folk had less tolerance than we have today. A few years ago it had fallen into a sad state of repair, but a lot of work has been done on it in recent times and its future now looks secure.

From the chapel a narrow road leads to Swinshaw Hall. Although this road runs parallel and just above the main A56 it is so peaceful and feels like a bit of real old England. The present hall dates only to 1870, but is a most impressive building and built on the site of an old half-timbered mansion which may well have been the starting point for the boar hunt.

The road then descends to and crosses the A56 before a futher incline leads to the valley of Limey water. A left turn then follows the stream through countryside once dominated by mills but which never lost its rural scenery. We have noticed that in the last few years the lichens have started to grow once more on the trees and walls in this area. Lichens used to be gathered and boiled in water to produce delicate if rather sombre dyes used to colour woollen clothes. Sometimes a chemical such as alum would be added to improve the dye. Such a chemical is called a mordant. Lichens do not grow well in polluted air, and when the mills were working flat out lichens disappeared altogether and have only recently started their come-back.

Swinshaw Hall built in the last century on the site of the hall from which the last boar hunt in England may well have started

Eventually a hump-backed bridge on the old packhorse route crosses Limey water and a path leads off to the right over the moors to Haslingden. In the days when the valley sides were full of trees and the bottoms flooded the only reliable trade routes kept to the well-drained hill tops. The view from the moorland is magnificent and must have provided the travellers of old with an idea of where the local thugs might try to attack and rob them.

Near the packhorse bridge is the animal cemetery where many pets have been laid to rest complete with memorial headstones. Almost on the bridge itself is a Quaker's Meeting House built in 1715 and which has a chair once used by the founder of the sect, George Fox. The building has been little altered and the stables where the friends kept their horses can still be seen. In those far off days the Quaker meeting house, and also Goodshaw Chapel, were in remote spots away from possible persecution.

Crawshawbooth has one final claim to fame. Ask any East Lancastrian where the Devil played his football and you will be told either Turf Moor or Ewood Park depending whether the supporter comes from Burnley or Blackburn. Legend has it, however, that Old Nick last turned out for a game one Sunday afternoon at Crawshawbooth. Apparently he played well until he kicked the ball so hard that it disappeared. Then one of the lads noticed the cloven hooves and forked tail. Old Nick then evaporated in a cloud of smoke and burning sulphur. These days they call it a free transfer!

The Quaker Meeting House near the packhorse bridge over Limey Water in Crawshawbooth

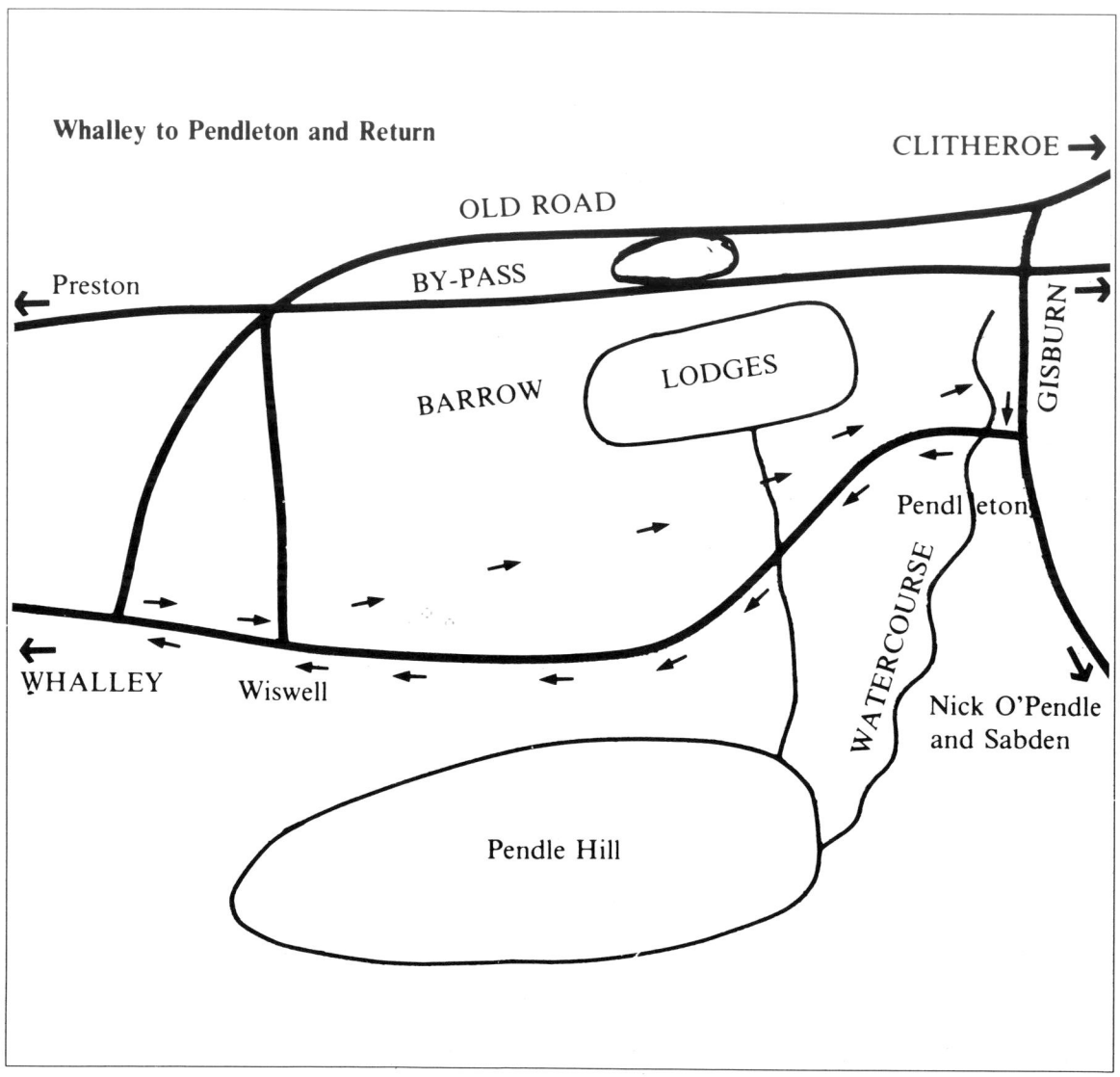

Whalley to Pendleton and Return

CLITHEROE →

OLD ROAD

← Preston

BY-PASS

BARROW

LODGES

GISBURN →

Pendleton

WATERCOURSE

← WHALLEY

Wiswell

Nick O'Pendle
and Sabden

Pendle Hill

Walk Thirteen

Whalley to Wiswell and Pendleton

ACCESS:

From Burnley follow the A671. At the traffic lights at Spring Wood take the filter left to Whalley and the car park is at the bottom of the hill.

From Preston and Blackburn follow the A59 to a roundabout at the Clitheroe bypass. Follow around the roundabout to the sign for Whalley. Follow the road through Billington, over Whalley bridge and through the village to the mini roundabout, turn right towards Burnley and then immediate right on to the car park.

ROUTE:

From the car park in the centre of Whalley, take the main road to Clitheroe (A59). About half a mile out take a right turn at Bramley Mead signed Wiswell. After crossing the Whalley bypass you will reach Wiswell. After exploring for a while find Cunliffe Lane. Find the footpath signed to Pendleton. Pass down a leafy lane and over a stream which can be quite damp after rain. Follow many stiles across lush fields. On the left you can see Barrow Lodges. The path is easily followed into Pendleton village. After exploring this lovely village find the signs indicating Wiswell and follow the narrow winding road which returns there. On this route are splendid old farms and cottages, with views of Pendle Hill at its most impressive. Just before reaching Wiswell is an attractive old Tithebarn. From Wiswell reverse the outward route to reach the car park at Whalley.

Allow 2-3 hours and even longer if you wish to take advantage of some pretty picnic spots. If you wish to shorten the walk it can be started either at Wiswell or at Pendleton.

OUR WALK:

Then meadow, grove and stream,
The earth and every common sight
To him did seem
Apparelled in celestial light
The glory and the freshness of a dream.

These words of William Wordsworth seem to us the perfect description of this walk, which in spring echoes to the song of the lark, in summer vibrates to the tune of buzzing bees, the autumn colours shine in the first frosts whilst in winter skeins of swans, geese and other wildfowl often fill the air with their wings' music.

The walk takes you through lush green meadows fringed with hawthorn, white in spring with its blossom and shining red with berries at the end of the year. Fieldfare and redwing gorge themselves with this harvest from the time of their arrival in September and October. Don't forget to do a little bit of bird nesting in the winter when old thrush and blackbirds' nests are taken over by long tailed field mice (also called wood mice) which store berries in them. These little mammals do not hibernate, and use these food stores when there is snow on the ground. They can be found also asleep in them when wet weather or melting snow makes life in their burrows impossible. A tiny stream meanders its way from the slopes of Pendle towards

Barrow Lodges and in its shallows, even in winter, lurk mayfly larvae, fresh water shrimps and water lice (relatives of the wood lice) finding food among the roots and fleshy leaves of water cress and the delicate crowfoot. Patches of colourful marsh marigold shine like sunlight during the productive months of May and June, and also part of this habitat are water voles, water shrews and the delightful pied wagtails which spend so much time around the streamside that in the old days they were called 'dishwashers'. This comes from the days of the old villages, when cottages had no running water and the village women wearing black dresses and white aprons washed the household dishes in the stream often in the company of the pied wagtails which are also spruced up in black and white plumage.

The Swan with Two Necks at Pendleton

Pendleton, one of the most attractive villages in Lancashire. It is cut in half by this pleasant little stream.

The village of Wiswell referred to in a charter dating back to 1193, is worth much more than a casual glance, and some of the cottages thereabouts have been tastefully coaxed to join the 20th century without losing touch with the 18th. At the end of a short lane from the village is an old farmhouse which was once, as its name implies, Wiswell Old Hall, and which deserves its place in history as the birth place of the ill-fated

John Paslew, the last Abbot of Whalley. During the reign of Henry V (early 15th century) Francis Paslew, who probably lived on the slopes of Pendle, bought the area around Wiswell and erected a modest, probably wooden, dwelling house, and a substantial structure was in existence by 1450. Francis had a son, John, who is thought to have been brought up in the hall prior to his preparation for a clerical life. Much of the present hall are later additions but the Paslew coat of arms, mullioned windows and the stone seats in the porch indicate its Tudor origins, as do the substantial chimneys. The climate hereabouts has always been mild and damsons grow well here, and in the months when the days are long the hedgerows are bursting with flowers, none more impressive than the white stitchworts and blue forget-me-nots shining out from the green of grasses and dog's mercury. In the damp areas bistort puts out its pink flowers. Bistort was once used in the treatment of high temperatures, and because of its smell has been called "the sweaty sock plant". At one time bistort was one of the constituents of Easter Ledger Pudding, a sort of herbal dish which was eaten to help women conceive and to protect them against miscarriage. Also used in the Ledger Pudding were nettle, dandelion and Lady's mantle, all of which can be found growing along the route followed by this walk. After passing down the delightful shaded pathway from Cunliffe Lane, it comes as a big surprise when you climb a stile and see before you the open fields seen at their best during early morning when the rising sun peeps over the broad beam of Pendle and glistens on the surface of the dew-strewn grass.

Pendleton is a delightful village, split in two by a tinkling, sparkling stream. It is mentioned in the Domesday book as a town at the foot of Pendle Hill. These days it is also famous for the public house with the unusual and apparently illogical name of *The Swan with Two Necks*. This dates back

The Red Necked Grebe is one of the rare species of bird which have been seen on the Barrow Lodges

centuries, when each of England's rivers had a ceremony called Swan-Upping. From the thirteenth century swans have been rounded up on the River Thames by those who were allowed to eat them by authority granted to them by the monarch. Any unmarked swan belonged to the Royal House, but those caught and scratched on the bill belonged to people influential enough to have been granted their own swan-mark. The oldest swan mark list in existence dates from 1482, but it is known that the Vintner's company were marking their birds with "two nicks", from the year 1472. The *Swan with two necks* is therefore an error by those who drew the Inn sign.

Pendleton is an ideal centre from which to explore the Clitheroe side of Pendle, and the views from the road to Wiswell are spectacular. Take an Ordnance survey map with you and pick out Longridge Fell, Pendle Hill and Moor, and Kemple End. Keep your eyes open, for there are many footpaths leading to all parts of Pendleside and this will give you, like us, the excuse you need to return to this area again and again. The Houghtons, of Houghton Tower, near Preston, had an association with Pendleton extending through nine generations before being succeeded by another influential local family, the Starkies, and their emblem the stork is commemorated in the name of a nearby house. Pendleton has many lovely old cottages, and Pendleton Hall retains the connection with the Houghton family. Here, then is the perfect walk full of history, natural history, historic public, domestic and manorial houses and the chance of a meal at the *Swan with Two Necks* and the *Freemasons' Arms* in Wiswell or one of the many hostelries in Whalley itself:

The brown trout (above) is a native species in the streams around Pendle, whilst fine specimens of the American rainbow trout (below) are often caught on Barrow Lodges

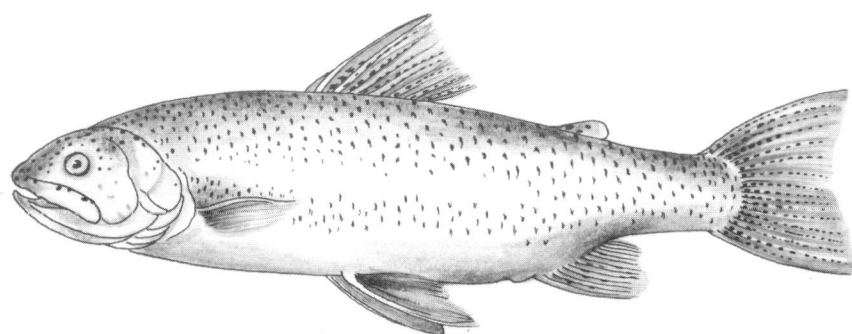

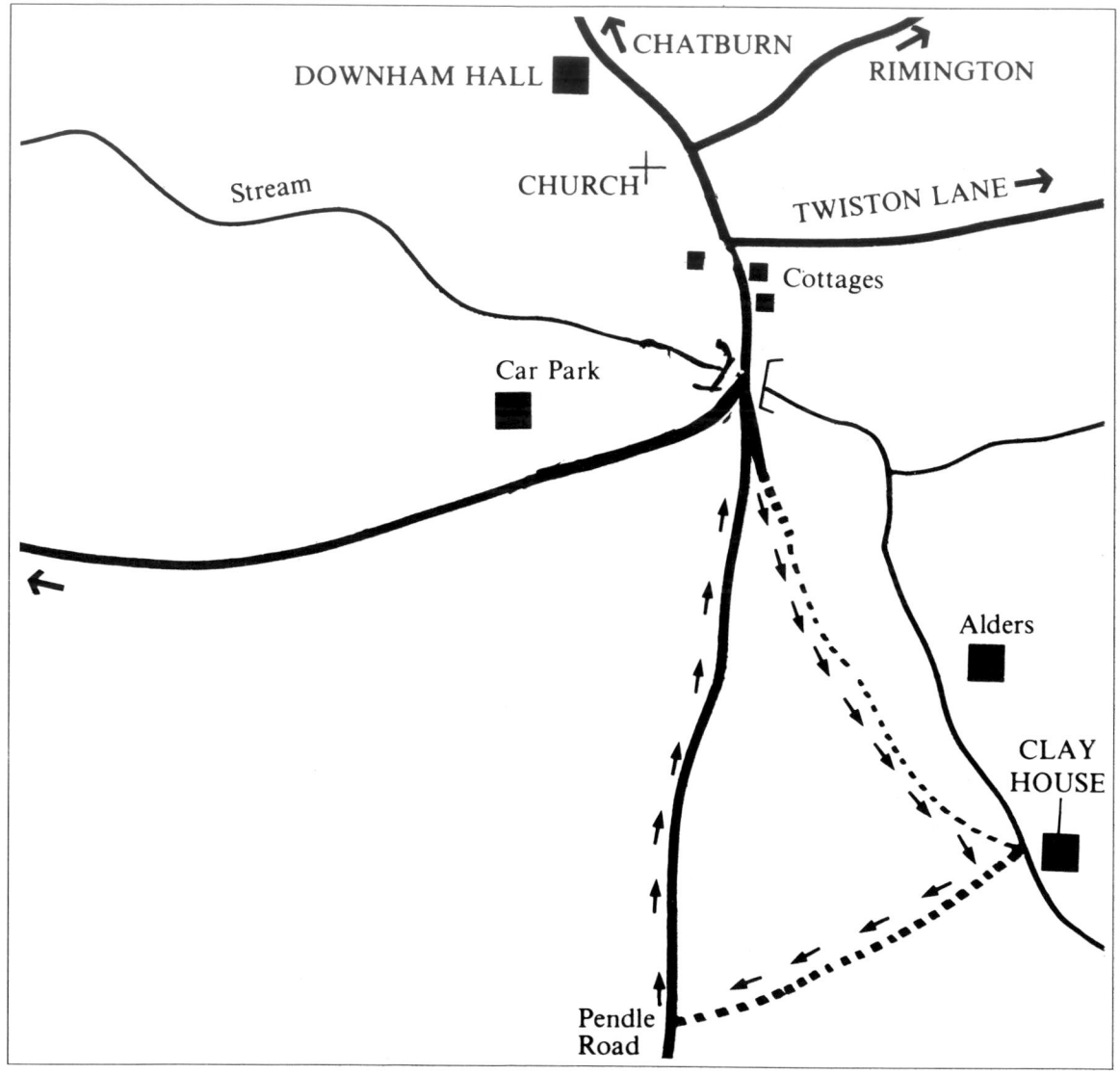

DOWNHAM HALL

CHATBURN

RIMINGTON

Stream

CHURCH

TWISTON LANE

Cottages

Car Park

Alders

CLAY
HOUSE

Pendle
Road

Walk Fourteen

Around Downham

ACCESS:

From Preston follow the A59 along the Whalley by-pass. Turn left, signed Chatburn. From Chatburn, Downham is indicated to the right. It can also be reached from Burnley via Barley and over the 'Big End' of Pendle.

THE ROUTE:

Once arrived in Downham, pass the church on the right, descend the hill, turning right over the bridge to the car park. Leaving the car park turn right before the bridge ignoring the road leading up towards Barley and keeping the water on your left. Pass splendid old cottages also on the left. Pass through a stile into fields and take the footpath leading to the right over a number of stiles. Pass a building on the left called the Alders. A footpath from here is labelled Clay House. Turn right from Clay House to reach the Barley road, which climbs over Pendle. The energetic may prefer to turn left and make the long slog to Barley. A less energetic diversion is first right and the left to Worston. The naturalist and historian, however, may well have spent too long in the village or hedgerow tohave time for either of these diversions. The road from Clay House to Downham is downhill all the way, but do spare the time to turn round and look at the spectaular views of dear old Pendle.

109

OUR WALK:

$1^{1}/_{2}$ – 2 hours, but longer for those who look and linger.

Arthur Mee, the famous geographer once described Downham as "like a bit of Elizabethan England forgotten by time." We do not wonder that the locals call it the prettiest village in Lancashire, and the magnificent views of Pendle have long excited walkers and strollers alike. Harrison Ainsworth the author of *The Lancashire Witches* put his feelings into words in a novel in which he has Nicholas Assheton utter the words "I love Pendle Hill and from whatever side I view it – whether from this place (Morton), where I see it from end to end, from its lowest point to its highest; from Padiham where it frowns upon me; from Clitheroe where it smiles; or from Downham where it rises in full majesty before me . . ."

Once you have strolled around the village, there are very few folk who would discount any of these claims. The whole area is one of our favourite haunts in winter, since that magnificent bird of prey the short eared owl can often be found on the local moorlands. It also breeds in the area and eats voles, shrews, mice and a few small birds, and to some extent it is a competitor of the red fox. It is around Downham that fox-hunting may well have had its beginnings. Squire Assheton had the good sense to keep a diary, and he describes the events of June 25th, 1617, in terms which make us feel that the survival of wildlife in the Pendle area must have been a major miracle. First he describes killing a bitch fox (the vixen) and then on the way home the good squire came across a Bowson, which is the old name for a badger. The poor beast was beset by terriers, then dug out and killed. The Squire's diary was quoted at length in *Kings of the Hunting Field* (Published in 1899), and is also mentioned in *English Fox Hunting, a History* by Raymond Carr

The red fox is a resident mammal around Downham.

(Weidenfeld and Nicolson 1976).

Downham, to us, has everything a good English village ought to have. It has a pretty stream full of vocal mallards (have a close look and you will find that only the females quack), wonderfully designed and maintained stone cottages, a church two centuries older than Whalley Abbey, a pleasant pub, stocks in front of an ancient sycamore tree, and thus abounds with both history and natural history. We suppose that the name Downham must almost be synonymous with that of the Assheton family. The pub now called the Assheton Arm,s was once named The "George and Dragon", but we have not yet met anyone who

111

would prefer to return to the old name. There has been a settlement hereabouts at least since Roman times, and one of three roads ran close by the present village. The manor of Downham was in the possession of a Saxon named Augrey, but true to his custom, William of Normandy rewarded his followers by liberal gifts of land. Ilbert de Lacey was granted Downham, and his family held it, not without trouble, until 1353 when the Duke of Lancaster, who had acquired it, gave it to the Dyneley family, who finally sold it to Roger Assheton in 1558. There the change ends and we are sure that the continual unifying presence of the family has kept this ancient settlement as a charming and relatively unspoilt village. We say relatively in the hope that we "townies" who descend upon it at weekends and holidays will take only photographs (and not flowers), leave only footprints (and no litter) and steal nothing but time!

Those with time to steal could do worse than find the old stocks opposite the Assheton Arms and beneath a gnarled old sycamore. The sycamore was not introduced into England from southern Europe on a large scale until the sixteenth century, but its broad leaves offer shade to the weary, nectar to the summer bees and shelter to the wintering starlings. Sycamore was a popular tree in Lancashire because it does not splinter easily and was therefore a safe timber from which to make the bobbins for cotton mills. Some sycamore trees, like this gnarled specimen which crouches like a dog at its master's feet, are of very ancient lineage. Across from the stocks and on the top of Downham stands the magnificent church gazing down and the lovely stone-grey village. The tower is fifteenth century and in it hang three bells which originally called the monks from Whalley Abbey to prayer. A further connection with Whalley is found within the church itself. Here is a font given by the last Abbot of Whalley, John Paslew.

Whatever I think of Downham these days two things spring to mind. Firstly, there are the ducks which seem to fill the village stream to overflowing and are usually to be seen delightedly gobbling up food brought by visitors. In late summer the ducklings brought by their mothers to the feeding station add extra charm to this rural scene. Secondly, we are reminded of that wonderful film made in black and white many years ago entitled *Whistle Down the Wind*, starring Hayley Mills, as a child. It was shot in the Downham/Worston area. In summer the village seems to be filled with the scent of sweet peas and roses, and, more materially, there is an added man-made bonus in the form of some very unusual door knockers on the cottages.

Passing over the bridge and bearing left between the old grey cottages, with their delightful country gardens, we reached the stile and moved across the fields. The stream in late summer and autumn is dotted yellow with clumps of monkey flowers. The corolla of this plant bears some resemblance to an ape, hence the name of Monkey flower. It is actually a native of North America, having been introduced into England as a garden plant in 1812. Quite soon it began to grow wild and is now common in all counties. Once, whilst walking here abouts, a tiny rusty-red bird with a short stubby tail flicked out from the overgrown bank and gave its alarm call which sound like a very fast tic-tic-tic-tic. It was a wren and there in a mossy bank we found a domed feather-lined nest containing five fluffy youngsters almost ready for flight. Wrens have an unusual method of nest building. The male builds several nests, sometimes as many as ten, and he then takes the female on a tour of inspection. She selects the one in which she will lay the eggs and only this one does she line with feathers. The others are not entirely lost, however, but may be used as comfortable roosts in cold weather. If the wrens do not use them then the long tailed field mouse

*The early purple
orchid grows
commonly along
the steam sides
around Downham*

may take over one of these "cock nests" for its winter home.

At all times of the year the pied wagtail finds food in the shallow stream or in the hedge bottom, and a majestic heron often raises on huge wings and heads off over Pendle. We remember in the wet spring of 1983 watching a young heron battle with an eel which, naturally enough, objected to being swallowed. When it had finished, the heron was covered in slime and we watched the wonderful way the bird gets rid of the stuff from its plumage. It bangs the sides of its body and the feathers there change into a soft material called "powder down". This is spread over the feathers and the slime is soaked up. All the heron needs then is a comb and one of its toes is so shaped. The slime is scraped off and flicked in to the water, after which the heron bathes and re-arranges its feathers. How spick and span it looked in the watery sunlight of that damp spring day.

Prominent features of much of our northern country-side are the wonderful stone walls full of ferns and fascinating plants. Just beyond Clay House we always stop to admire the growth of ivy-leaved toadflax. Often called Wandering Sailor and also Mother of Thousands, this charming plant arrived as a garden plant in the seventeenth century and deliberate plantings and escapes have ensured its rapid spread. It has one unique feature which helps it to thrive on walls. Once the flower head has died the seed capsules grow away from light, which means they literally turn around and grow into cracks inside which the seeds can easily germinate. Its original home was in the Mediterranean, and its snap-dragon-like flowers are pollinated by bees, some of which are on the wing during early April. Its scientific name is *Cymbalaria muralis* – muralis meaning wall. The stems have large numbers of leaves, each of which is lobed like ivy but are depressed in the centre rather like a cymbal from which the scientific name was derived. In Italy the plant is called *Madonna's Flower*, but it certainly thrives well on the stone walls of Pendleside and on those of Downham, one of its most beautiful villages.

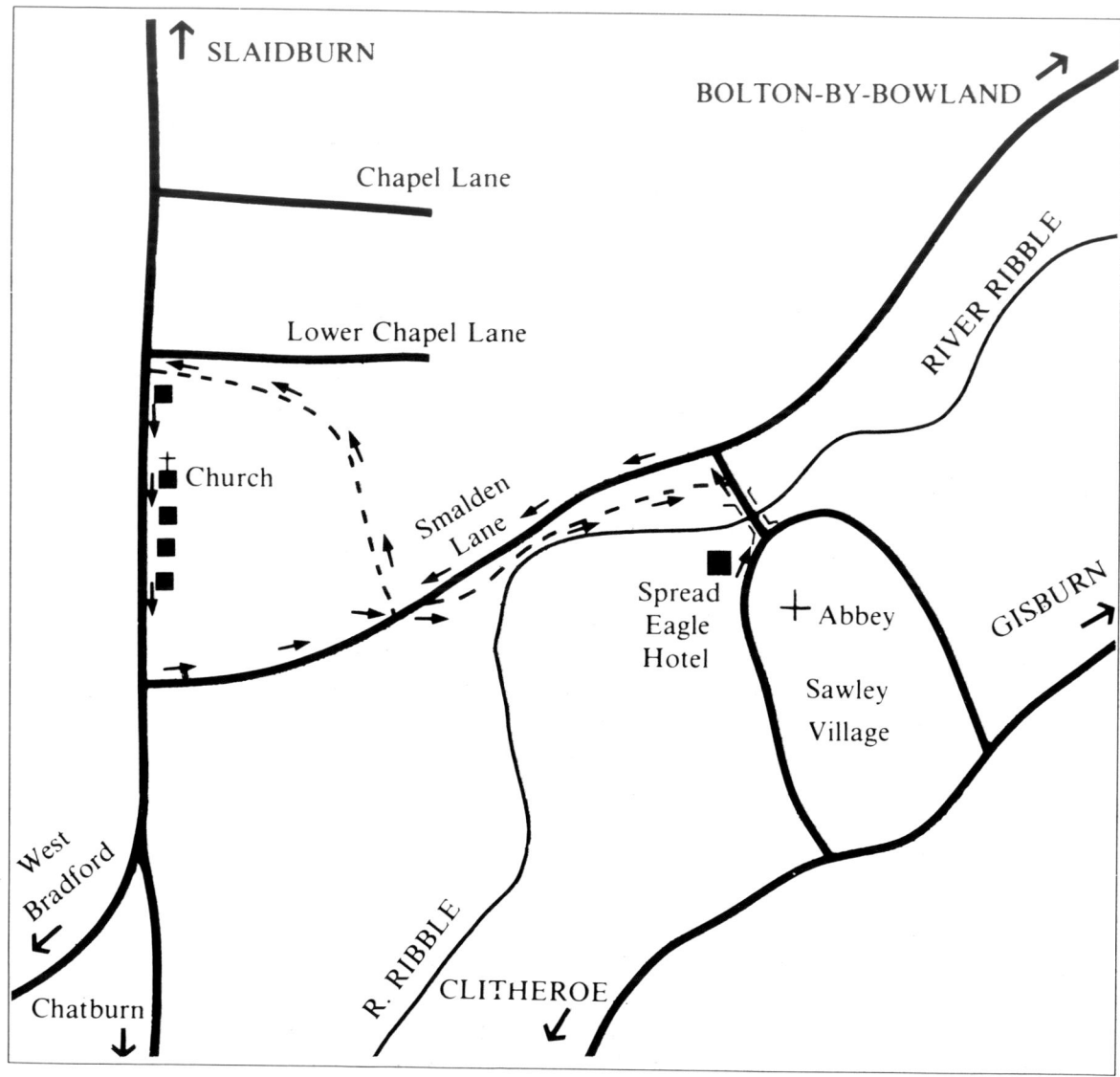

Walk Fifteen

Sawley to Grindleton and return

ACCESS:

From the Preston area follow the A59 passing signs for Clitheroe and following the signs to Skipton. Just past Chatburn, Sawley is signed to the left and there is parking in the vicinity of the Ribble near the Spread Eagle Hotel.

THE ROUTE:

Begin at Sawley (Salley) Abbey. Turn left at the Spread Eagle Hotel. Cross Sawley Bridge and follow the road towards Grindleton. Climb a steep hill, passing a house called Foxley Bank on the right. On the right near the crest of the hill find a signpost indicating Smalden lane. This climbs pleasantly and offers leafy views of Pendle and the River Ribble meandering gently in its green valley below. Pass the church of St Ambrose and explore the lovely village of Grindleton. Take the road out towards Sawley (and Bolton-by-Bowland.) This leads over a lovely field and ends at Sawley Bridge. Beyond the bridge is the Abbey and your starting point.

THE WALK:

This is a walk of about 3 miles but there is plenty to see and so allow at least 3 hours.

Sawley is a lovely village on the banks of the River Ribble and would be worth its place in the annals of Pendleside

The Spread Eagle Hotel at Sawley has cellars which suggest that they may once have been the undercroft of the old Cistercian Abbey

even without the impressive grandeur of what remains of the once proud Cistercian Abbey. The white monks raised Salley abbey to the glory of God on land given William, the third Baron Percy, in the year 1147. Benedict, the first abbot, brought his brethren from the mother abbey at Fountains, who with their usual brilliant foresight found a sheltered fold in the river to build their home. Especially in the early years of the monastic movement some splendid scholars were produced and perhaps Salley's brightest star was William de Rymington, who became Chancellor of Oxford University and was very vigorous in attacking the ideas of John Wycliffe at the time of the great religious upheaval which we now call the Reformation.

As with all these walks this trip can be enjoyed whatever the season, whatever the weather, but it is truly magnificent during May. You pass close to one of Britain's cleanest rivers, with its soft damp water meadows, along roadsides lined with stone walls and roadside trees, up narrow leafy lanes and alongside a churchyard. A combination of all these factors ensures a great variety of plant life and those interested in botany will find much to fascinate them. Wood sorrel, primrose, bluebell, dog's mercury, forgetmenot, sweet cecily and Jack-by-the-Hedge fill every nook and cranny during May, and wild garlic fills the air with its onion like aroma. This smells strongly enough to make your eyes water when the sun shines on it just after rain.

On one memorable August night, with a real harvest moon shining from a starry sky and shooting stars lighting up the sky like November 5th, we followed this route. Bats swooped low over the Ribble, a hare charged off and actually cleared a stone wall with one bound, but our real treasure was lurking up Smalden Lane. We heard him first, snuffling among the hedge parsley, and then out he came into the path and outlined in bright moonlight was a splendid boar badger, to be followed a few seconds later by his mate. During the summer months badgers can forage some distance from their setts in search of a change of diet, or perhaps to get some peace from their cubs which are getting large and playful at this time. What a joy it was to see them.

The badger has the scientific name of *Meles meles* and it has been present in Britain for over 14 million years, with fossils found in most counties. A look at old maps and a study of the place names often show where badgers were common in the old days. The ancient name of brock was used a long time before badger, and names such as Brockholes, Brockley, Brockmoor and Brockbank are good examples. In Wales the animal is called mochyn bychan, which means earth-pig. In French the word for digger is becheur, from which we get the name badger, no doubt brought over by the Normans. We still have badgers locally, which is nice, and we also have people who bait badgers even though it is against the law; which is not so nice. The "sport" of

Somerset House once stood at the junction of the old Turnpike road ascending Sawley Brow. Since the opening of the new road the old Turnpike has been reduced to a farm track.

badger baiting involves catching a live animal and placing it inside a barrel laid on its side. Dogs are then encouraged to fight the badger and money is won by the owner of the most courageous terrier. Many of these game little dogs are badly maimed and to even up the contest the badger is often beaten with iron bars or sticks and its teeth and jaws broken.

Grindleton is a pretty village winding like a ribbon up to the hills and affording magnificent views over the Ribble Valley and beyond it Pendle Hill. Good old Pendle has dominated the scenery of each part of this walk, but it is from Grindleton that the whole length of the hill is seen in all its splendour. The name of the village almost certainly indicates that it was the site of sacred fires kindled by the folks who lived hereabouts before the arrival of the Saxons. Here then may well have been the home of the Druids and those who worshipped the sun and may have practiced human sacrifice, but whose knowledge of herbal law was profound and used for good as well as evil purposes. The heather has long since left this peaceful village and the church of St Ambrose is now in charge of the spiritual part of the village.

Each British plant has its own history, but we have lived in towns or been dependent upon them for so long that we often forget the reliance which our ancestors placed on them. In the water meadows by the Ribble the springtime walker will find the Mayflower. This belongs to a family of flowers called Cruciferae. They all have four petals arranged in the form of a cross. The vernacular names including cuckoo flower. It is one of the first plants to come into bloom in damp meadows and is often found about the same time as the first cuckoo calls. In height it varies between 9 inches and 15 inches (23-38 cms) and the flower may be pale violet or white. This lovely plant has many other names up and down the country, including shoes and socks, cuckoo's shoes and stockings, Lady's smock, nightingale's flower, water lily, bog spink, May blob, milk maid, ladies' glove, ladies' cloak and over fifty others. In some parts of England this plant is also called the cuckoo flower. This is why we need to use scientific names in order to avoid confusion.

It is not only the plants which make this a wonderful walk. Birds are always present and curlews announce the arrival of spring, skylarks soar above the green fields and lapwings are found in every season. In winter the views are even more spectacular, as the bridge at Sawley comes into view with the snow laden hills behind. At these times small flocks of goosander are often seen on the river. The monks did not seem to appreciate our local climate and complained of bitter winters and wet summers. More than 600 years have gone by since then and things seem much the same! Perhaps the monks felt worse because they had no time to stroll in the countryside, no thermal underwear or efficient waterproofs, and neither had they a warm house to return to. Modern life has something to make us thankful about after all.

Since it was protected in the 1970s the badger population has increased dramatically in Lancashire

Other books to look out for in this series –

SONGS OF
A Lancashire Warbler
by
Lowell Dobbs

Hoo seet mi heart gooin' back an' forrit,
Thumpin' like a facthry mule-
Then hoo spun her charms areawnd it
Like silk areawnd a spool.

£4.95

LANCASHIRE 150 YEARS AGO

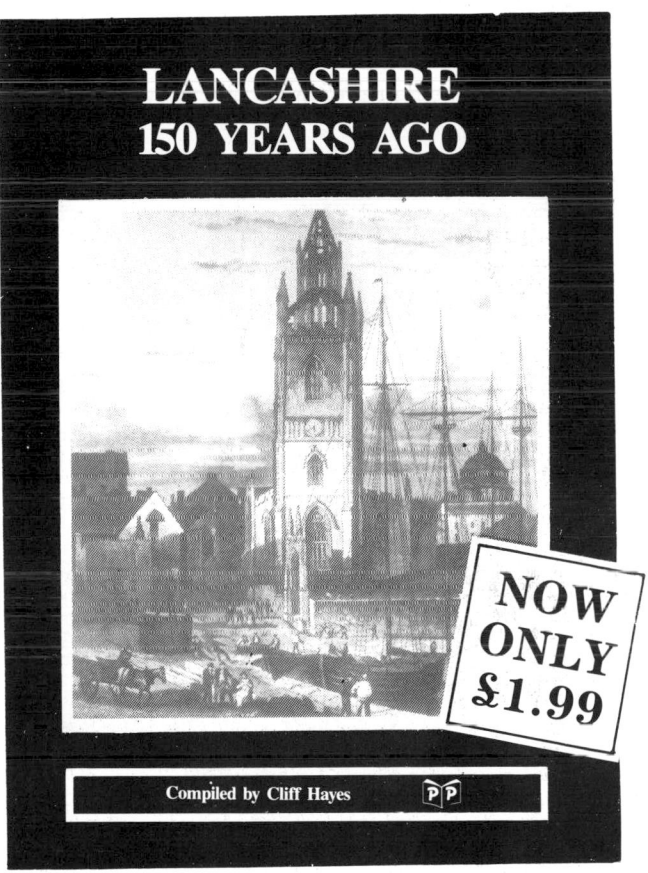

A great addition to the collection of any lover of Lancashire's history

OTHER LOCAL PUBLICATIONS

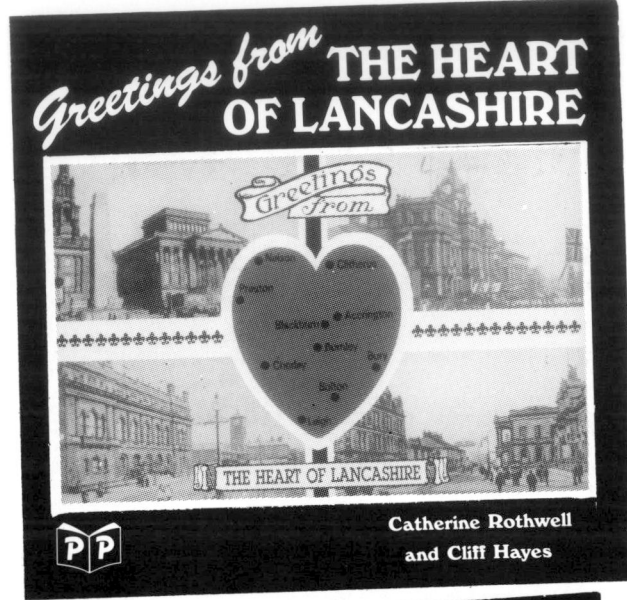

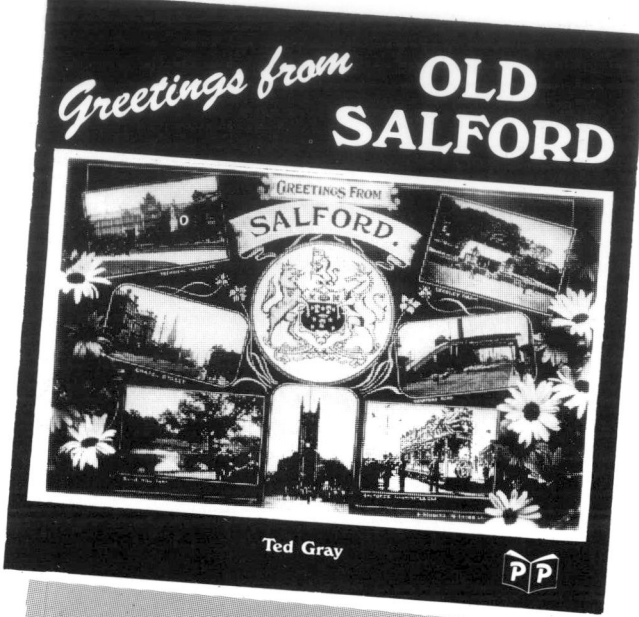

ALSO NORTH WALES; ECCLES; AROUND MANCHESTER; LIVERPOOL

The History of Lancashire Cookery

by Master Chef Tom Bridge

Printwise Publications Limited

Well known Master Chef Tom Bridge turns his attention to his home county. As each recipe takes us deep into Lancashire's culinary past he reveals the history and the tales which surround the classic dishes of the region.

This book is dedicated to Her Royal Highness the Princess Anne. A donation will be made from the royalties of this book to the Save the Children Fund, Princess Anne's favourite charity.

Includes a facsimile reprint of the U.C.P. Tripe Recipe Book from 1934.

NORTHERN CLASSIC REPRINTS

The Manchester Man

(Mrs. G. Linnaeus Banks)

Re-printed from an 1896 illustrated edition — undoubtedly the finest limp-bound edition ever. Fascinating reading, includes Peterloo. Over 400 pages, wonderfully illustrated.

ISBN 1 872226 16 7   £4.95

The Manchester Rebels

(W Harrison Ainsworth)

A heady mixture of fact and fiction combined in a compelling story of the Jacobean fight for the throne of England. Manchester's involvement and the formation of the Manchester Regiment. Authentic illustrations.

ISBN 1 872226 29 9   £4.95

Hobson's Choice (the Novel)

(Harold Brighouse)

The humorous and classic moving story of Salford's favourite tale. Well worth re-discovering this enjoyable story. Illustrated edition. Not been available since 1917, never before in paperback.

ISBN 1 872226 36 1   £4.95

More Stories Of Old Lancashire

(Frank Hird)

We present another 80 stories in the same easy, readable style, very enjoyable, great. With special section for Preston Guild 1992.

ISBN 1 872226 26 4   £4.95

Stories & Tales Of Old Lancashire

(Frank Hird)

Over 70 fascinating tales told in a wonderful light-hearted fashion. Witches, seiges and superstitions, battles and characters all here.

ISBN 1 872226 21 3   £4.95

Poems & Songs Of Lancashire

(Edwin Waugh)

A wonderful quality reprint of a classic book by undoubtedly one of Lancashire's finest poets. First published 1859 faithfully reproduced. Easy and pleasant reading, a piece of history.

ISBN 1 872226 27 2   £4.95

The Best of Old Lancashire — Poetry & Verse

Published in 1866 as the very best of contemporary Lancashire writing, this book now offers a wonderful insight into the cream of Lancashire literature in the middle of the last century. Nearly 150 years later, edited and republished, the book now presents a unique opportunity to read again the masters of our past.

ISBN 1 872226 50 7   £4.95

The Dock Road

(J. Francis Hall RN)

A seafaring tale of old Liverpool. Set in the 1860s, with the American Civil War raging and the cotton famine gripping Lancashire. Period illustrations.

ISBN 1 872226 37 X   £4.95

The Lancashire Witches

(W. Harrison Ainsworth)

A beautifully illustrated edition of the most famous romance of the supernatural.

ISBN 1 872226 55 8   £4.95

Stories Of Great Lancastrians

(written Frank Hird)

The lives of 24 great men of the county, told in easy reading style. Complete with sketches and drawings, a good introduction to the famous of Lancashire and Manchester. John Byrom, Arkwright, Tim Bobbins, Duke of Bridgewater.

ISBN 1 872226 23 X   £4.95